THE USBORNE

TIME TRAVELER

Judy Hindley, Anne Civardi, James Graham-Campbell,
Heather Amery, Patricia Vanags and Tony Allen

Edited by Philippa Wingate
Illustrated by Stephen Cartwright and Toni Goffe
Designed by Michèle Busby and John Jamieson
Series Designer: Russell Punter
Consultants: Vivienne Henry and Dr. D. M. Wilson

Contents

FIRST STOP

KNIGHTS & CASTLES

Contents

YOUR FIRST JOURNEY IN TIME

Time travel is easy when you have a magic helmet. All you have to do is put it on, press the right buttons, and you are off.

Throughout Europe you can still see the castles where wealthy barons and their knights lived. But these real castles are often empty and half ruined. With your time travel helmet, you can see how a castle looked with a fire roaring in the hearth and people chatting in the candlelight.

For your first journey through time, you are going to use your magic time helmet to travel back more than 750 years, to a castle owned by a nobleman named Baron Godfrey.

1. YOUR TIME HELMET

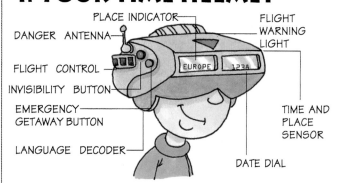

Here is the magic time travel helmet. It has lots of useful gadgets, including a Language Decoder, a Danger Antenna and an Invisibility Button.

2. YOUR DESTINATION

Set the Place Indicator to "Europe" and the Date Dial to "1238". Below are a few stop-off points to show you how things change when you jump back in time.

3. GO!

This is northwest Europe in 1940. Notice that both the plane and the radio look different. Like most families at this time, this family doesn't have a television.

Now you have gone back another 40 years and things are quite a bit different. There are gas lamps, lots of decorations, and the women wear long skirts.

You have jumped back another 300 years. The room is lit by candles. There isn't much furniture and the window is made of tiny panes of glass.

You have reached 1238, your first destination in time. The room you find yourself in has no glass in the windows and there is no chimney for the fire.

THE PEOPLE YOU WILL MEET

The castle you are going to visit in this book belongs to Baron Godfrey. It is in northwest Europe.

Everyone you will meet has special duties, whether they are peasants or barons. Baron Godfrey, for example, must serve the king, and be a strong leader who protects the people that live on his land.

PEASANT

Most peasants farm the land or work as craftsmen. They pay rent to a local baron to live on his land.

MEN-AT-ARMS

Men-at-arms are ordinary fighting men. They fight on foot, because only knights fight on horseback. Barons have men-at-arms to defend their castles.

NUN   MONK

Monks and nuns are people who have promised to serve God by work and prayer, and sometimes by teaching and helping people.

PRIEST

BISHOP

A priest is a religious man who works in a church. A bishop is in charge of many priests.

FRIAR

A friar is a priest who doesn't have a church. He travels around teaching and preaching.

SERF

Serfs are like slaves. They work for the local baron and pay rent to live on his land.

BARON GODFREY AND HIS FAMILY

The main people you will meet on your journey are Baron Godfrey, his family and friends. They live together in his castle.

BARON GODFREY   LADY ALICE

The Baron is a knight and a nobleman. He is the lord of many less powerful knights. He owns a lot of land, a castle and several houses. His wife is Lady Alice. One of her duties is to teach the young girls in the castle to read, write and sew.

SIMON

Simon is Godfrey's son. He will soon be a knight. Knights fight on horse-back. They are usually the sons of important people.

ROBERT

Robert is Godfrey's nephew. He is a squire, which is a trainee knight. It is his job to work for his cousin Simon.

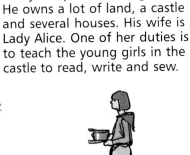

PETER

Peter, Baron Godfrey's steward, is the head of all the servants. He can read and write, and do large sums.

SERVANT

Godfrey has many servants who must obey his wishes. They live in the castle with the Baron and his family.

JOURNEY TO A CASTLE

Your time helmet has brought you to Europe in the year 1238. You are outside Baron Godfrey's castle. All the land you can see belongs to the Baron. All the people who live here work for him and obey him.

In return, the Baron and his knights protect them from criminals and enemies.

The Baron owns several homes. Today he is taking his family, his knights and his servants to visit his castle.

They will live at the castle and eat all the food grown on its land. When the food runs out, they will move on to another one of his houses.

THE SERFS IN THE VILLAGE CAN ONLY LEAVE IF THEY BUY THEIR FREEDOM FROM THE BARON, OR ESCAPE TO A BIG TOWN.

ANIMALS AND PEOPLE STILL DO MANY KINDS OF HARD WORK LIKE PREPARING THE FIELDS FOR CROPS.

THIS IS A WATER MILL. THE STREAM TURNS THE WHEEL, WHICH TURNS A HEAVY STONE. THE STONE GRINDS WHEAT INTO FLOUR.

THE ROAD IS A ROUGH AND DANGEROUS PLACE TO BE AS THERE ARE MANY ROBBERS.

BARON GODFREY

LADY ALICE

LADY ALICE'S BEST CANDLESTICKS

BARON GODFREY TAKES ALL HIS VALUABLES WITH HIM FROM HOUSE TO HOUSE, IN CASE ONE OF HIS HOMES IS CONQUERED WHILE HE IS GONE.

THE CARTS TRAVEL SLOWLY, ONLY ABOUT 30KM (19 MILES) A DAY.

4

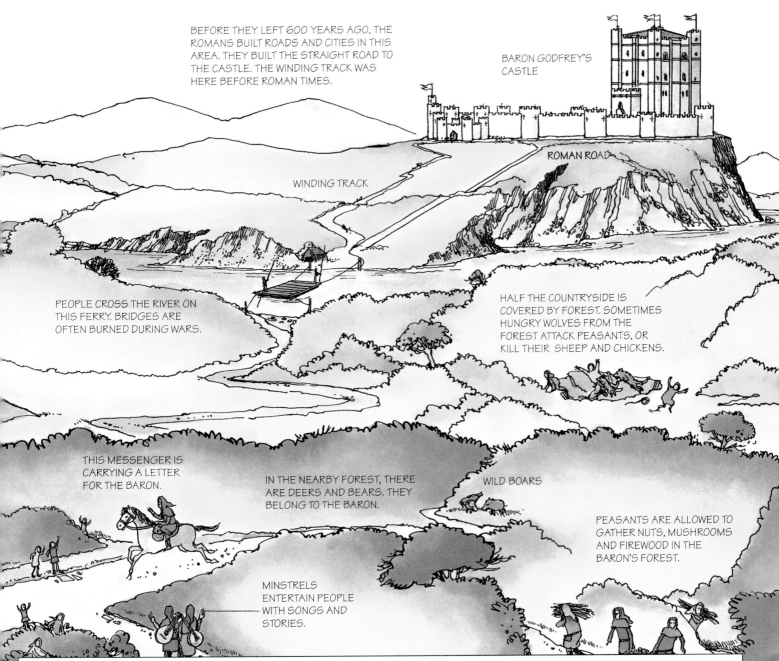

BEFORE THEY LEFT 600 YEARS AGO, THE ROMANS BUILT ROADS AND CITIES IN THIS AREA. THEY BUILT THE STRAIGHT ROAD TO THE CASTLE. THE WINDING TRACK WAS HERE BEFORE ROMAN TIMES.

BARON GODFREY'S CASTLE

ROMAN ROAD

WINDING TRACK

PEOPLE CROSS THE RIVER ON THIS FERRY. BRIDGES ARE OFTEN BURNED DURING WARS.

HALF THE COUNTRYSIDE IS COVERED BY FOREST. SOMETIMES HUNGRY WOLVES FROM THE FOREST ATTACK PEASANTS, OR KILL THEIR SHEEP AND CHICKENS.

THIS MESSENGER IS CARRYING A LETTER FOR THE BARON.

IN THE NEARBY FOREST, THERE ARE DEERS AND BEARS. THEY BELONG TO THE BARON.

WILD BOARS

PEASANTS ARE ALLOWED TO GATHER NUTS, MUSHROOMS AND FIREWOOD IN THE BARON'S FOREST.

MINSTRELS ENTERTAIN PEOPLE WITH SONGS AND STORIES.

BY LAND AND BY SEA

Many of the people you will meet on the road are pilgrims. These are religious people who travel the land, visiting holy places.

It is not very safe to travel by road. Many merchants have their goods stolen by robbers who lie in wait for them.

Travel by sea is dangerous too. Sailors steer their ships by the stars and try to keep close to land whenever they can.

INSIDE THE CASTLE WALLS

In some parts of Europe, powerful barons are fighting each other for land. Each baron tries to gather as many knights as he can and build the strongest castle.

This is Baron Godfrey's castle. The safest part of the castle is the tower in the middle called the keep.

The keep has no doors or windows near the ground. Behind it is a steep cliff which nobody can climb and in front of it are two walls and a ditch. To get to the keep people have to pass through four separate gates.

Inside the castle it is like a little town. There are tailors, carpenters and blacksmiths. So if the castle was attacked, the people inside could live comfortably for weeks.

DOOR TO WALL WALK

DOVE COTE

ARCHERS PATROL THE WALLS. THEY CAN SHOOT ENEMIES THROUGH SLOTS IN THE WALL.

SENTRIES

KENNELS

HAY STACKS

PORTCULLIS

GATEHOUSE

DRAWBRIDGE

DOUBLE DOOR

SERVANTS LIVE IN THESE HUTS.

BEGGARS

THE BARON ARRIVING

THE BARBICAN IS AN EXTRA GATEHOUSE OUTSIDE THE CASTLE'S DITCH. IT PREVENTS ENEMIES COMING STRAIGHT UP TO THE CASTLE GATE.

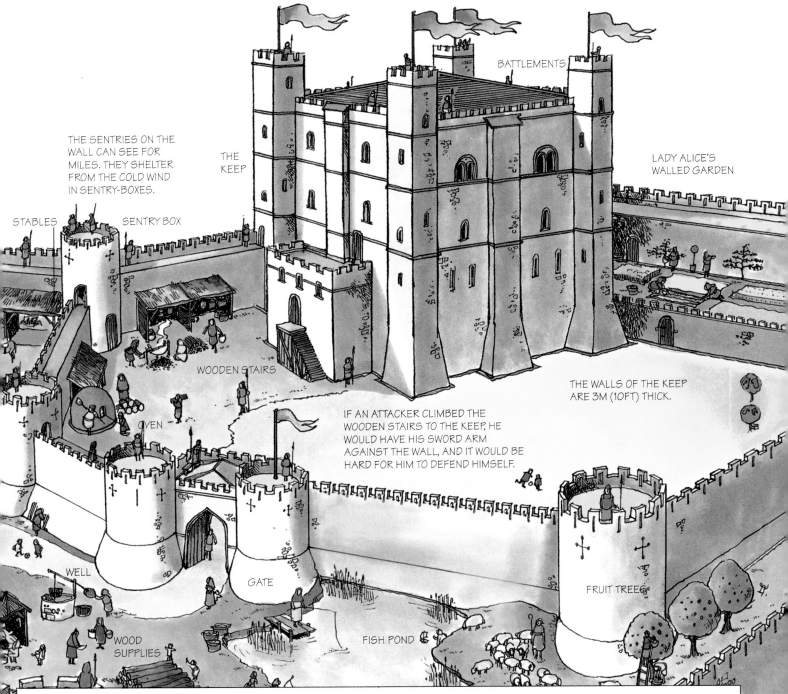

THE SENTRIES ON THE WALL CAN SEE FOR MILES. THEY SHELTER FROM THE COLD WIND IN SENTRY-BOXES.

BATTLEMENTS

THE KEEP

LADY ALICE'S WALLED GARDEN

STABLES

SENTRY BOX

WOODEN STAIRS

OVEN

THE WALLS OF THE KEEP ARE 3M (10FT) THICK.

IF AN ATTACKER CLIMBED THE WOODEN STAIRS TO THE KEEP, HE WOULD HAVE HIS SWORD ARM AGAINST THE WALL, AND IT WOULD BE HARD FOR HIM TO DEFEND HIMSELF.

WELL

GATE

FRUIT TREES

WOOD SUPPLIES

FISH POND

ENTERING THROUGH THE CASTLE GATES

DRAWBRIDGE IS LOWERED

GATE OF BARBICAN

GATEHOUSE

BOLT

PIT

PORTCULLIS

To enter the castle, a visitor first has to pass through a gatehouse called the barbican. This is outside the castle's ditch.

Next, a drawbridge is lowered and bolted in place. The entrance is still defended by an iron grill called a portcullis, and big double doors.

When the portcullis is opened, it slides up grooves in the walls. Finally, the doors are unbolted and the visitor can enter the castle.

THE KEEP

This is the keep of the castle, where the Baron lives with his family and friends, his knights, his men-at-arms and his servants.

In the courtyard, there are many traders. Meanwhile, in the rooms upstairs, Lady Alice and her companions are busy sewing, weaving and embroidering. One of them is being entertained by a troubadour. This is a knight who travels around, singing songs and reciting poems. Sometimes, religious men called friars visit the castle to preach and read from the Bible.

THIS WOMAN IS WEAVING A TAPESTRY.

TROUBADOUR

THIS MAN IS REPAIRING THE ROOF.

THESE MEN ARE MAKING POTS THAT WILL BE USED IN THE KITCHENS.

BARON GODFREY

DUNGEON

SALT MERCHANT

PETER

STAIRCASE

PILGRIM

SALT IS USED TO PRESERVE MEAT THROUGH THE WINTER.

THESE MEN ARE ARGUING ABOUT A STOLEN PIG. PETER THE STEWARD IS LISTENING TO THEM. HE IS A LIKE A POLICEMAN. HE WILL PUNISH THE CRIMINAL.

TINY ROOMS AND PASSAGES ARE CUT INTO THE KEEP'S THICK OUTER WALLS.

THIS MAN IS ON GUARD DUTY.

IN THE GARDEN, LADY ALICE GROWS FLOWERS AND FRUIT. HERBS SUCH AS MINT, THYME, FENNEL, PARSLEY, SAGE AND HYSSOP ARE GROWN FOR COOKING AND MEDICINES.

THE BARON'S ROOM

BABY

BEAMS

THE TOILET IS JUST A HOLE IN THE WALL.

FRUIT TREES

THE CHAPEL

THE GREAT HALL

FOOD AND DRINK ARE KEPT IN THE STOREROOMS IN CASE THE CASTLE IS ATTACKED.

THESE WOMEN ARE DOING THE LAUNDRY. THEY BOIL THE CLOTHES TO GET THEM CLEAN.

STOREROOM

THESE MAIDS ARE LOOKING AFTER THE BARON'S CHILDREN.

RECORDS ARE KEPT OF WHATEVER FOOD GOES IN AND OUT OF THE STOREROOMS.

THE WOMEN MAKE THEIR OWN SOAP.

THESE CLOTHES ARE DRYING IN THE SUN.

9

DAWN AT THE CASTLE

A huge bell is rung to wake everyone up.

MEN-AT-ARMS

THIS MAN IS ASLEEP ON THE JOB.

SEVERAL SERVANTS AND THE BARON'S DOGS SLEEP IN THE SAME ROOM AS THE BARON'S FAMILY.

THE BARON'S BED IS FILLED WITH STRAW. IT HAS CURTAINS TO MAKE IT SNUG AND PRIVATE.

RUSHES AND STRAW MAKE THE FLOOR FEEL WARMER. SERVANTS SWEEP THEM OUT WHEN THEY GET DIRTY.

NIGHT LIGHT

THE ONLY WAY TO THE TOP OF THE KEEP IS UP THE SPIRAL STAIRCASE.

MOST PEOPLE SLEEP ON PALLETS. THESE ARE MATTRESSES STUFFED WITH STRAW OR FEATHERS.

A DANCING BEAR

PEOPLE AT MORNING PRAYERS

THE SERVANTS WAKE EARLY TO LIGHT THE FIRES AND START COOKING BREAKFAST.

THERE IS NO COFFEE OR TEA, FEW PEOPLE LIKE MILK AND PLAIN WATER CARRIES GERMS. SO EVEN CHILDREN DRINK BEER.

10

BARON GODFREY GETS DRESSED

Before the Baron gets up, he puts on his shirt.

Next, he washes with cold water and soap.

He puts on his long tights, which are called hose.

His leather shoes fasten up with a button.

The Baron's robe is lined with fur to keep him warm.

A useful bag for coins slides onto his belt.

LADY ALICE GETS DRESSED

Lady Alice puts on her long wool tunic.

On top of this she wears a robe called a surcoat.

A maid carefully braids Alice's long hair.

She coils the braids around Alice's ears.

The maid ties a piece of cloth over the braids.

Finally, she places a hat on top of the cloth.

AND OTHERS GET DRESSED

Monks and nuns spend their lives serving God and helping people. They wear long, plain clothes.

Young girls do not wear their hair in braids.

From an early age, boys carry daggers in their belts.

Servants wear plain, sensible clothes.

On wet days, servants wear wooden clogs.

TAKING A BATH

This morning Robert the squire is taking a bath. Servants fill a big wooden tub with hot water. This takes a long time, so Robert shares his bath with friends. The servants sprinkle the water with flowers because the soap doesn't smell very nice.

THESE LADIES ARE BUSY GOSSIPING.

FLOWERS

A BOWL OF SOAP

BELLOWS TO MAKE THE FIRE BURN

BUCKETS OF HOT WATER

THE SOAP IS MADE OF ANIMAL FAT, ASH AND SODA. IT IS SOFT AND SQUASHY.

GOING HUNTING

Baron Godfrey and Lady Alice are out hunting. They hope to catch a stag. They set out early, riding through the woods and fields. It is a sunny day, and everyone is in very good spirits. They are singing songs and laughing.

A group of local peasants are hiding among the trees. They have been stealing pheasants to eat. If caught, they will be punished.

It is almost dark when the hunters finally catch the stag. To celebrate, one of the hunters plays his horn while the animal is killed.

THIS MAN IS BLOWING ON A HUNTING HORN, MADE FROM A STAG'S ANTLER. IT ONLY PLAYS ONE NOTE.

THE PEASANTS DON'T LIKE THE HUNTERS. THEIR FIELDS AND CROPS ARE OFTEN DAMAGED BY THE HUNT, AND THEY MAY BE FORCED TO GIVE REFRESHMENT TO THE HUNTERS FROM THEIR OWN SMALL SUPPLIES OF FOOD.

SOME HUNTERS CARRY CROSSBOWS.

LADY ALICE HOLDS A FALCON.

THESE TERRIFIED PEASANTS ARE HIDING BEHIND A TREE.

TRAINING A FALCON TO HUNT

People train falcons to hunt other birds. When it is young, the trainer feeds the bird by hand. He wears a thick glove so the bird can perch on his wrist.

HOOD

When the falcon is tame, the trainer attaches a bell to its foot, and ties a leash to a ring on its leg. To keep the bird calm, the trainer puts a hood over its head.

HOUNDS AND THEIR KENNELS

A keeper looks after the hounds. Every day, he sprinkles their kennels with fresh straw. At night, a boy sleeps alongside them to keep them quiet.

BY EVENING THE HUNTERS ARE TIRED, MUDDY AND SORE, BUT THE SOUND OF THE HORN LEADS THEM ON.

THIS MAN IS CELEBRATING THE KILL.

THIS MAN IS KILLING THE STAG WITH HIS KNIFE.

The trainer lets the falcon fly short distances on its leash. He whistles to bring it back, and rewards it with food. Later, the bird learns to hunt without a leash.

If the hunt is successful, the trainer finds the falcon by following the sound of its bell. He takes the prey away and rewards the falcon with a piece of raw meat.

13

A TRIP TO A BUILDING SITE

This morning, Baron Godfrey and Lady Alice are visiting the place where a new church is being built. Carpenters, blacksmiths, roofers, glass-makers and stone workers called masons, are all busy at work.

Throughout Europe, craftsmen are finding new ways to build bigger and better churches and cathedrals. A large church, or cathedral, can take as long as 50 years to finish. Even a small church like this one will take about seven years to complete.

BARON GODFREY AND LADY ALICE ARRIVE ON HORSEBACK.

BOYS, KNOWN AS APPRENTICES, DO ERRANDS AND DIRTY WORK. IN EXCHANGE, THEY GET A HOME, FOOD, AND LESSONS IN THEIR CRAFT FROM OLDER CRAFTSMEN.

THIS MAN IS MAKING A SUBSTANCE CALLED MORTAR OUT OF SAND, WATER AND LIME. IT IS USED TO STICK STONES TOGETHER.

SAND

APPRENTICE

CHISEL

BUCKETS OF MORTAR

CRAFTSMEN FROM OTHER COUNTRIES COME TO FIND OUT NEW WAYS OF WORKING. THESE TRIPS ARE CALLED WANDER-YEARS.

MASONS USE HAMMERS AND CHISELS TO CARVE DECORATIONS IN THE STONES.

GUIDELINES FOR WALLS

PATTERN

EACH MASON USES A SPECIAL MARK, SUCH AS A STAR OR CROSS, TO SIGN HIS WORK.

UNDERNEATH THE CHURCH WALLS IS ANOTHER SET OF WALLS THAT REACH DEEP UNDERGROUND. THESE HELP TO SUPPORT THE HEAVY BUILDING.

BUILDERS USE PATTERNS TO SHAPE THE STONES TO FORM AN ARCH. EACH STONE IN AN ARCH IS WEDGE-SHAPED, SO THAT IT PRESSES ON THE STONE BENEATH IT.

THIS WOODEN FRAME WILL BE COVERED WITH TILES OR LEAD SHEETS.

PULLEY

THIS MAN TURNS A WHEEL ATTACHED TO A ROPE TO RAISE AND LOWER HEAVY STONES.

ARCH

PILLAR

THIS IS THE ARCHITECT WHO DESIGNED THE CHURCH.

THE WORKERS BUILD SCAFFOLDING TO STAND ON AS THE WALLS GET HIGH.

EVERY BLOCK OF STONE HAS TO BE BROUGHT TO THE SITE BY HORSE AND CART. IT IS HARD, SLOW WORK.

15

A TRIP TO TOWN

Baron Godfrey's steward, Peter, is riding into town. Lady Alice has given him a huge shopping list. She needs wax candles, red dye for her new dress, and some spices and silks brought from foreign countries.

The town is an exciting place to visit. There are lots of craftsmen and merchants. They belong to organizations called guilds. The guilds ensure that their members trade honestly and do their work well. They hold meetings in a building called the guildhall, and have their own badges and songs.

CRIMINALS ARE HANGED ON THE HILL.

THE GUILDHALL

THE PILLORY

A MAN HAS BEEN PUT IN THE PILLORY FOR SELLING STINKING FISH.

THE BARBER SHOP. THE BARBER IS ALSO THE DENTIST AND THE SURGEON. HE TREATS THE SICK BY CUTTING THEM TO MAKE THEM BLEED A LITTLE.

NUNS LOOK AFTER POOR, SICK PEOPLE IN THE HOSPITAL.

THIS RIVER IS THE TOWN'S MAIN WATER SUPPLY.

A GATE KEEPER SHUTS THESE GATES AT NIGHT TO KEEP OUT THIEVES.

THE GOLDSMITH'S SHOP IS WELL PROTECTED.

PETER

16

THE TOWN IS FILTHY. PIGS AND BIRDS EAT FOOD THAT IS LEFT ON THE STREETS.

THE CHURCH

TOWN SQUARE

EACH MARKET STALL OWNER HAS TO GET PERMISSION TO TRADE FROM THE TOWN COUNCIL.

THE CHURCH IS ALWAYS BUSY. PEOPLE COME TO GOSSIP AND PRAY. A HUNTED CRIMINAL IS SAFE FROM ARREST IF HE STAYS NEAR THE ALTAR.

THIS PILGRIM IS VISITING A SAINT'S TOMB IN THE CHURCH. HE WEARS A CROSS ON HIS BACK.

PEOPLE GROW FOOD IN THEIR GARDENS.

A TEACHER AND HIS PUPILS

THE MERCHANTS WHO LIVE IN THE TOWN RENT THE LAND FROM A LORD KNOWN AS JOHN DEADTOOTH.

WATCHMEN WALK THE STREETS AT NIGHT WITH LANTERNS. THEY CRY "CURFEW". THIS MEANS PEOPLE MUST COVER THEIR FIRES. THE WOODEN HOUSES CATCH FIRE EASILY.

GIVING A FEAST

Today is an important festival day and the Baron is giving a feast.

In the kitchen, the servants have been working since dawn. Food is often scarce in winter. Some years ago, during a famine, the local peasants had to eat grass. But today, the servants are preparing lots of splendid food.

They cook meat and vegetables, and add herbs and spices to make them taste good.

THIS WOMAN IS GRINDING UP HERBS AND SPICES WITH A PESTLE AND MORTAR.

GEESE FROM THE POULTRY YARD

THIS BOY IS TURNING A SPIT. HE USES AN OLD ARCHERY TARGET AS A FIRE SCREEN.

SPIT

CAULDRON

MEAT IS ROASTED ON A SPIT IN FRONT OF THE FIRE.

PAN TO CATCH MEAT JUICES

BAKING BREAD

A fire is lit inside the oven to heat it while the dough is being made. Then the fire is raked out and the dough popped in to bake as the oven cools.

After the bread is baked, the oven will be used to make cakes or even to dry clothes or to dry wood for the fire. Every bit of heat is used.

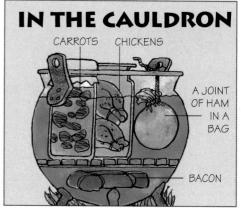

IN THE CAULDRON

CARROTS   CHICKENS

A JOINT OF HAM IN A BAG

BACON

This picture shows some of the things that might be cooked in a cauldron. Later, the hot water will be used for washing up. Nothing is wasted.

IN THE GREAT HALL

At noon, the tables in the great hall are laid. The Baron's guests include friends, traders and wandering knights. Everyone loves being entertained with music, games and stories.

There will be four courses of food served today. Here are some of the dishes: boar's head; shellfish with jasmine, rosemary and marigold; salmon with creamy sauce; spiced beef; stuffed quarter of bear; sugared mackerel; squirrel stew and cakes with honey.

THESE TABLES ARE MADE OUT OF BOARDS RESTING ON TRESTLES.

TRESTLE —

THE BARON AND LADY ALICE SIT AT A SPECIAL RAISED TABLE, CALLED THE HIGH TABLE.

"Let no man laugh at us discomfited, But pray to God that he forgive them all."

MINSTRELS

BOAR'S HEAD

MYSTERY PLAYS

On special holidays, like today, the members of each of the guilds act out scenes from the Bible. These are called mystery plays.

The performers stand on wagons called pageants, which they move around to different parts of the town between the performances.

Many people can't read, so the plays help them to get to know Bible stories. The guild which does the best play wins a prize.

ROBERT, THE SQUIRE

Robert is the Baron's nephew. He was sent to stay with his uncle when he was six years old. For many years, he has lived at the castle, learning to be obedient

When he was 14 years old, Robert became a squire. This means that he began training to be a knight. Robert also works for the Baron's son, Simon, who will soon become a knight.

Here are some of the things squires learn.

1. USING A CROSSBOW

ROBERT CAREFULLY TAKES AIM.

TEACHER

A CROSSBOW

LOADING A CROSSBOW

ARROWS

LOOP

The young squires have to learn how to load and fire a crossbow. Although knights never use their crossbows in battle, they do use them when they go hunting.

Crossbows are very difficult to load. A squire has to put one foot into a loop at the base of the bow, and then pull hard with both hands to fix an arrow in place.

2. RIDING

Robert has to learn how to ride one-handed. This keeps his weapon arm free. He trains his horse to get used to loud noises, so it doesn't bolt during a fight.

3. USING A LANCE

QUINTAIN

LANCE

Here Robert is about to gallop at a rotating target, called a quintain. He has five tries to knock it down by hitting it exactly in the middle.

He holds the heavy lance against his side to keep it steady. It is important to aim the lance very carefully, otherwise it will throw him off-balance when it strikes.

At the last moment, he rises in his stirrups to get his whole body behind the blow. If the blow is off-target, the quintain will swing around and hit him.

4. SWORD PLAY

ROBERT

Here, Robert and another young squire are using small, blunt swords made of wood, and little round shields called bucklers.

Robert learns to slash with the sword's edge and catch blows from his opponent with his sword or the buckler.

As the boys get stronger, they use heavier weapons. A real battle sword weighs 1.5kg (3.5lbs), and it can slice through steel.

20

A SQUIRE'S DUTIES

A squire has to help a knight get dressed for jousts and battles.

He has to help the knight put on his chain mail shirt.

He cleans rusty chain mail by rolling it in a barrel of sand.

AT SCHOOL

A priest teaches the squires how to read and write. Sometimes Lady Alice reads to them, and tells them stories of famous people.

The boys don't have paper to write on. They use pointed sticks and tablets covered in wax. They have an abacus (a frame with wires along which balls slide) to do calculations.

PRIEST

ABACUS

LADY ALICE

THE YOUNG SQUIRES PLAY GAMES

When they have finished their lessons and their duties, the young squires can enjoy some fun and games. They pretend to fight with wooden swords and wrestle with each other.

Some of the boys have made a toy horse from a tree trunk. They have attached four wooden wheels to it. They use it to learn how to hold a lance and hit a target.

SIMON BECOMES A KNIGHT

The time has come for Simon to become a knight. His training is complete. He and several of his friends will be knighted at a grand ceremony in the great hall of the castle.

First, they spend the whole night praying in the chapel. They don't eat or sleep all night. They ask God to help them when they are knights, because they must be good, strong and fearless.

They wear long white robes. This is a sign that they promise to be pure and faithful when they are knights.

All night, the young men stay in the chapel. They lie on the floor to pray. It is freezing cold!

After praying all night, Simon takes a bath in preparation for the important ceremony.

With Robert helping him, Simon puts on his white robe and takes his precious sword.

Now Simon goes down to the great hall for the ceremony at which he will become a knight.

22

THE CEREMONY

Before Simon is knighted, his squire, Robert, dresses and arms him for battle. When he is ready, Baron Godfrey will make him a knight.

1. A quilted vest and cap will help protect Simon from swords and arrows.

2. His heavy chain mail shirt is very slippery and it is difficult to put on.

FASTENING

3. Chain mail is made of linked metal rings. Simon's shirt has a special hood.

4. Robert fastens the leather straps which hold Simon's chest protector. It is made of metal plates.

5. When he is on horseback, a knight wears metal shin guards and mail leggings for protection.

6. He has arm guards and shoulder guards to shield him from an enemy's slashing sword.

7. He wears a linen tunic over his chain mail to stop it from getting rusty in the rain.

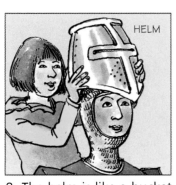

HELM

8. The helm is like a bucket, with holes in it for seeing and breathing. It hides his head completely.

9. He wears a symbol called a coat-of-arms on his tunic, his shield and his shoulder guards, to show who he is.

10. A priest blesses Simon's sword. A sword is shaped like a cross, and shows a knight's devotion to God.

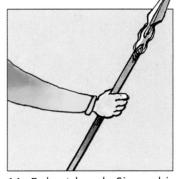

11. Robert hands Simon his lance. Lances are used to fight at tournaments.

Awake from evil dreams. Keep watch faithful in Christ, and praiseworthy in fame.

12. The Baron strikes Simon on both shoulders with the flat side of a sword.

13. Simon has been "dubbed" a knight. Now he can wear his spurs.

14. One day, Simon will be able to dub new knights himself.

GOING TO A TOURNAMENT

Baron Godfrey has arranged a tournament to celebrate Simon's knighthood. Knights will fight mock battles, known as jousts.

Suddenly, the trumpeters play a fanfare to announce the arrival of the Black Knight.

He is a knight errant, which means that he goes from tournament to tournament hoping to earn prize money. If he wins a joust, he gets his opponent's horse and weapons. Today, Simon has challenged the Black Knight

to a joust. He hopes to prove his skill as a fighter.

Simon's squire, Robert, is at his side, ready to help in any way he can.

The field is crowded. People have come for miles around to enjoy the sports.

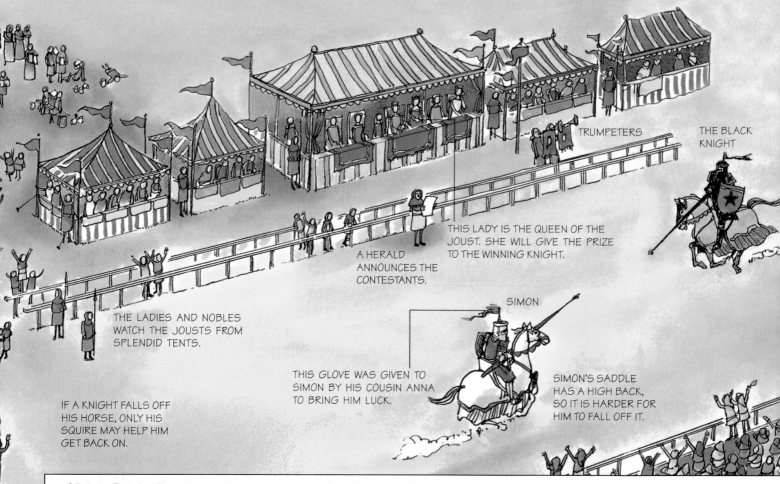

TRUMPETERS

THE BLACK KNIGHT

THIS LADY IS THE QUEEN OF THE JOUST. SHE WILL GIVE THE PRIZE TO THE WINNING KNIGHT.

A HERALD ANNOUNCES THE CONTESTANTS.

THE LADIES AND NOBLES WATCH THE JOUSTS FROM SPLENDID TENTS.

SIMON

THIS GLOVE WAS GIVEN TO SIMON BY HIS COUSIN ANNA TO BRING HIM LUCK.

SIMON'S SADDLE HAS A HIGH BACK, SO IT IS HARDER FOR HIM TO FALL OFF IT.

IF A KNIGHT FALLS OFF HIS HORSE, ONLY HIS SQUIRE MAY HELP HIM GET BACK ON.

SIMON FIGHTS THE BLACK KNIGHT

The trumpet sounds. This tells the knights their contest has begun. Simon digs his spurs into his horse's sides. If he manages to strike the top of the Black Knight's helmet, he will win his first point.

On the first charge, Simon's lance is shattered. But each knight can use three lances before he is defeated.

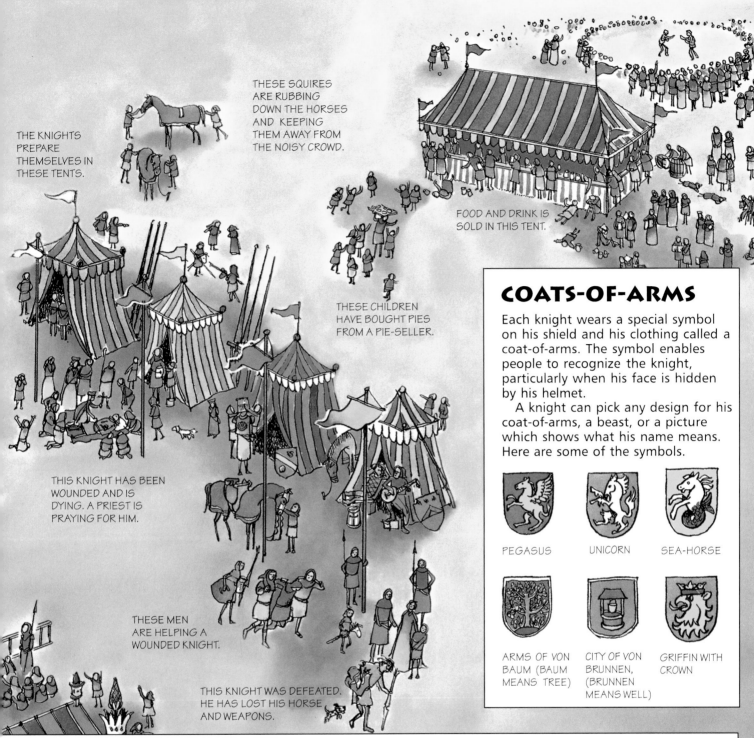

THE KNIGHTS PREPARE THEMSELVES IN THESE TENTS.

THESE SQUIRES ARE RUBBING DOWN THE HORSES AND KEEPING THEM AWAY FROM THE NOISY CROWD.

FOOD AND DRINK IS SOLD IN THIS TENT.

THESE CHILDREN HAVE BOUGHT PIES FROM A PIE-SELLER.

THIS KNIGHT HAS BEEN WOUNDED AND IS DYING. A PRIEST IS PRAYING FOR HIM.

THESE MEN ARE HELPING A WOUNDED KNIGHT.

THIS KNIGHT WAS DEFEATED. HE HAS LOST HIS HORSE AND WEAPONS.

COATS-OF-ARMS

Each knight wears a special symbol on his shield and his clothing called a coat-of-arms. The symbol enables people to recognize the knight, particularly when his face is hidden by his helmet.

A knight can pick any design for his coat-of-arms, a beast, or a picture which shows what his name means. Here are some of the symbols.

PEGASUS

UNICORN

SEA-HORSE

ARMS OF VON BAUM (BAUM MEANS TREE)

CITY OF VON BRUNNEN, (BRUNNEN MEANS WELL)

GRIFFIN WITH CROWN

When both knights have broken all their lances, they dismount and continue the contest with swords.

The Black Knight is knocked down. He is at Simon's mercy. Simon can hold him prisoner if he wants to.

But Simon decides to release him. Simon's only request is to exchange horses as a reminder of the fight.

RETURN FROM THE CRUSADES

One day, a procession appears at the castle gates. There are weary men, and donkeys laden with heavy packs filled with strange trees, silk cloth and exotic gifts. With them is a creature that nobody in the castle has ever seen before – a camel.

The men look strange. Their clothes and saddles look foreign. Suddenly, Lady Alice realizes that one of these men is her brother, Rudolf. For four years he has been in Jerusalem fighting a religious war called a crusade.

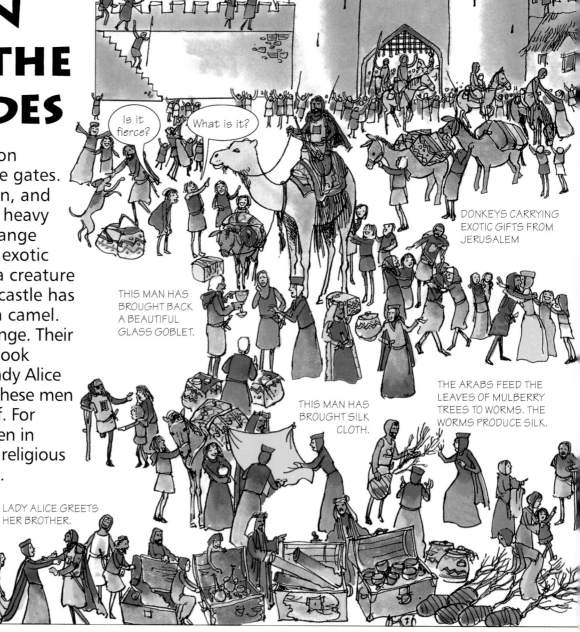

Is it fierce?

What is it?

DONKEYS CARRYING EXOTIC GIFTS FROM JERUSALEM

THIS MAN HAS BROUGHT BACK A BEAUTIFUL GLASS GOBLET.

THIS MAN HAS BROUGHT SILK CLOTH.

THE ARABS FEED THE LEAVES OF MULBERRY TREES TO WORMS. THE WORMS PRODUCE SILK.

THIS MAN HAS BROUGHT AN APRICOT TREE BACK FROM THE HOLY LAND.

LADY ALICE GREETS HER BROTHER.

WHAT IS A CRUSADE?

A crusade is a religious war. The most famous crusades were wars in which Christian armies from Europe tried to conquer Jerusalem and the holy places where Jesus lived. They started in 1095.

For centuries, Christian pilgrims visited Jerusalem. They were treated well by the Arabs who ruled there. The Arabs were Muslims.

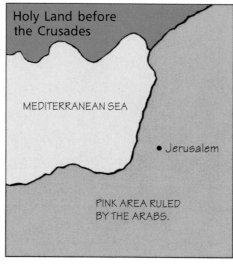

Holy Land before the Crusades

MEDITERRANEAN SEA

• Jerusalem

PINK AREA RULED BY THE ARABS.

This means they followed the teachings of the Prophet Mohammed. But they respected the beliefs of the Christians, and made them welcome.

In the 11th century, the Arabs were conquered by a group of people called the Seljuk Turks. They took control of the Holy Land. The Seljuk Turks were also followers of Mohammed.

TELLING TALES

Lady Alice's brother tells of his adventures on crusade.

But they were less sympathetic toward the Christians. They made them pay vast sums of money to see the holy city of Jerusalem.

Meanwhile, in Europe people had begun to want the goods that were brought from the Holy Land – such as spices, which they used in their cooking. For many reasons they became very angry with the Turks.

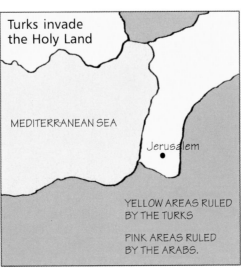

The Pope, the head of the Christian Church, decided that Christian armies must fight for Jerusalem. This was the first crusade.

For over 200 years, the crusades continued. Jerusalem was won by the Christians and then lost again. In the end, it stayed in the hands of the Muslims.

THE CASTLE IS ATTACKED

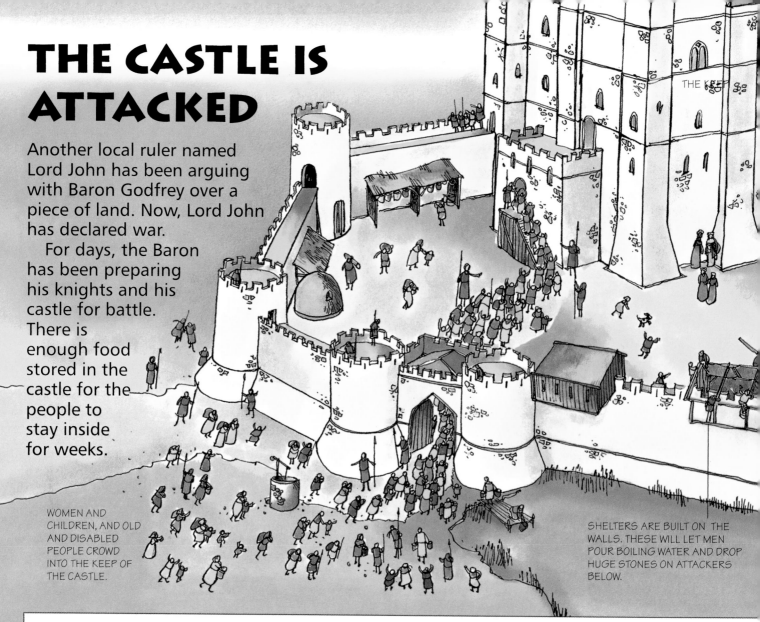

Another local ruler named Lord John has been arguing with Baron Godfrey over a piece of land. Now, Lord John has declared war.

For days, the Baron has been preparing his knights and his castle for battle. There is enough food stored in the castle for the people to stay inside for weeks.

THE KEEP

WOMEN AND CHILDREN, AND OLD AND DISABLED PEOPLE CROWD INTO THE KEEP OF THE CASTLE.

SHELTERS ARE BUILT ON THE WALLS. THESE WILL LET MEN POUR BOILING WATER AND DROP HUGE STONES ON ATTACKERS BELOW.

SIEGE WEAPONS

In a siege, an army surrounds a castle, trapping its occupants inside. The people inside the castle can survive until their food and water runs out; then they have to fight, surrender or die from starvation.

During a siege, both the attacking army and the people inside can use weapons to try to win more quickly. Here are some of the siege weapons they use.

SIEGE TOWER

The attacking army can roll a huge wooden tower, called a siege tower, against the castle wall. Then, they can climb up it and go over the wall.

An army can dig a tunnel under a castle wall. They prop the tunnel up with wooden supports. If they burn the supports, the wall above collapses.

LORD JOHN ATTACKS

By the second day of fighting, Lord John's men have dug a tunnel under the castle wall. The wall crumbles and the Baron's men have to retreat into the keep.

VICTORY!

That night, Simon and a band of knights creep out of a secret gate at the back of the keep. Silently, they set fire to the enemy's camp. Lord John's men flee. In the final battle, many men are killed. The Baron himself is wounded; but the castle is saved.

Attackers can batter down the walls with heavy logs or battering rams with metal points.

Hiding behind wooden shields called mantlets, attackers can carry ladders up to the castle. They use these to climb over the walls.

ARROW SLITS

CROSSBOWS

The archers defending a castle shoot their arrows through slits in the wall. These protect their bodies from enemy arrows.

THIS ARCHER IS USING A LONGBOW.

An archer, using a bow called a longbow, can reload much more quickly than if he uses a crossbow. This means he can fire more arrows.

A CASTLE MAP

Now instruct your time travel helmet to allow you to hover high above Europe. You will be able to see where the finest castles are found in 1238.

NORWAY

Akershus

FINLAND

Abo

SWEDEN

Visby

ESTONIA

LATVIA

DENMARK

Hammershus

LITHUANIA

Drum

Craigmillar

Alnwick

Carrickfergus

BRITAIN

Conisbrough

HOLLAND

Marienburg

BELARUS

IRELAND

Trim

Carlow

Ferns

Caernarvon

Harlech

Chepstow

Castle Rising

Muiden

Leyden

GERMANY

POLAND

Caerphilly

Tower of London

Chateau des Comtes

Markesburg

Eltz

Coburg

Bezdéz

CZECH REPUBLIC

Karlotejn

UKRAINE

Restormel

BELGIUM

LUXEMBOURG

Arques

Falkenstein

Ortenberg

Araberg

SLOVAKIA

MOLDOVA

Chateau Gaillard

Gisors

La Roche Guyon

AUSTRIA

HUNGARY

Coucy

Etampes

Pfeffengen

Viechtenstein

Angers

SWITZERLAND

Chillon

Kropfenstein

Trento

SLOVENIA

ROMANIA

Langeais

Loches

FRANCE

Fenis

Sirmione

Castelveccio

CROATIA

BOSNIA-HERZO-GOVINA

Golubac

YUGOSLAVIA

Villandraut

Aigues Mortes

Gradara

Sarzanello

San Gimignano

BULGARIA

Carcassonne

ITALY

ALBANIA

MACEDONIA

Roumeli Hissar

Anadoli Hisa

Burgos

Villalonso

Castel Sant Angelo

Castel del Monte

GREECE

Amiera

Avila

SARDINIA

Castle Nuovo

Lisbon

SPAIN

Bellver

Monte Agudo

Palermo

Catania

CRETE

PORTUGAL

SICILY

TUNISIA

MOROCCO

ALGERIA

HOW CASTLES GREW

A castle is a fortress that people lived in, protected from their enemies. There are castles all over the world. Some are still lived in; some are now museums. Many castles are in ruins.

The first kind of castle in Europe was a low tower with a hall, in which people lived, built above storerooms.

People often had to build castles quickly, so they used wood. Motte-and-bailey castles, like the one below, were common.

MOTTE

BAILEY

The "motte" was a mound. The "bailey" was a fenced-off area. These were sometimes replaced by stone castles later.

KRAK DES CHEVALIERS

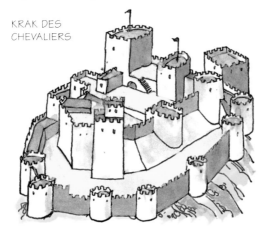

By the time of the crusades, people were building beautiful castles, such as Krak des Chevaliers in Syria.
Many castles were built with several circles of walls, one inside the other. These were called concentric castles. Others had towers along their walls, called mural towers.

CAERPHILLY, A CONCENTRIC CASTLE

The way in which a castle was constructed often depended on where it was built. For example, in mountainous areas, a castle might be just a tower built on a rocky peak. Some castles were built on islands in the middle of lakes. Many castles became the luxurious homes of noblemen.

COUCY, IN FRANCE

TURKEY

Krak Des Chevaliers

CYPRUS

SYRIA

KNIGHTS & CASTLES
TIME QUIZ

1. What is the tower in the middle of Baron Godfrey's castle called?
2. How many prisoners can you see in the dungeon at Baron Godfrey's castle?
3. What is the name given to a knight who travels around singing songs and reciting poems?
4. What does Baron Godfrey keep in the bag which hangs from his belt?
5. What is the name given to boys who are learning a particular craft or trade?
6. Can you find a man with a cross on his back on page 16 or 17. Who is he?
7. What does the barber do as well as cut hair?
8. What is a quintain?
9. Knights have special symbols on their clothing and shields. What are the symbols called?
10. What city did the Crusaders try to conquer back in the Holy Land?

Answers on page 130.

NEXT STOP

VIKING RAIDERS

Contents

BACK TO VIKING TIMES

Now you must leave Baron Godfrey's castle and travel further back in time.

For your second journey you are going to visit Norway in the year 890. This is during a period known as the Viking Age, when ferocious sea raiders terrorized people all over Europe.

To get there, you need to go back nearly 350 years in time. But with your magic helmet it will only be a few seconds before you are hovering over Norway, ready to come face-to-face with a band of Viking warriors.

Once you are there, you will be able to find out all about their homes, their lives and their adventures overseas. You will join them at a feast and watch them sailing to Greenland.

1. SET YOUR TIME HELMET

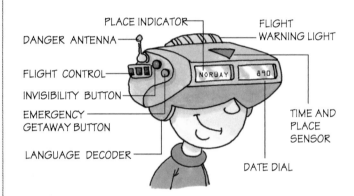

To make sure you arrive at your new destination safely, you need to adjust the controls on your time helmet.

Set the Place Indicator to "Norway" and the Date Dial to "890".

2. YOUR DESTINATION

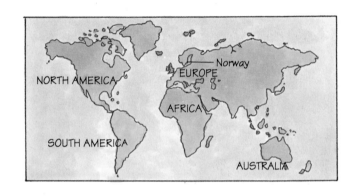

Norway is a country in northern Europe. It is one of the countries that make up the area we now call Scandinavia.

Below you can see the castle you are leaving behind and the settlement you will arrive at.

3. GO!

One moment you are in the castle, watching Baron Godfrey's wife weaving a tapestry. A minstrel is singing songs for her and playing his lute. The next moment you are off, whizzing through space. The Flight Warning Light on your helmet flashes as you travel 350 years back through time.

Now you have arrived at your destination. The first thing you notice when you look around you is that the houses people live in have changed.

The Vikings don't live in castles. They build their houses from stones or wood, depending on what they can find. They cover the roofs with thatch.

THE PEOPLE YOU WILL MEET

The Vikings you will meet in this book live in Norway. Vikings live in Sweden and Denmark too. Life is hard for them, because the winters are long and cold, and it is difficult to grow good food.

The main people you will meet are a powerful chieftain named Knut, and his family. Knut leads a band of fierce warriors. During the summer, they sail across the sea to raid and loot other countries.

All Vikings are freemen. This means that nobody owns them. Freemen who don't own land, work on farms that belong to wealthy Vikings. They tend crops, build ships and go raiding.

MAGNUS

Magnus is the most important freeman on Knut's farm. He is a blacksmith. As well as weapons for the raiders, he makes tools and pots and pans.

Slaves are men and women who are captured on raids. Knut has 12 slaves. They do all the dirty work.

OLEG

Oleg is learning to be a blacksmith. He helps Magnus in the smithy. His bad temper often gets him into trouble.

KNUT AND HIS FAMILY

Knut is the most important chieftain in this part of Norway. Raiding has made him very rich and he owns a lot of land.

KNUT

ASTRID

Astrid has been married to Knut for 24 years. When she was younger, she went with him on raiding expeditions. Now, she stays at home and looks after the farm. Astrid is always busy spinning, weaving or cooking.

HALFDAN

SVEN

BJÖRN

Halfdan is 22 years old. He is the eldest son, and will take over his father's farm when Knut dies. Halfdan is famous for his skill as a swordsman.

Sven, the second son, is 21. He is wild and brave, and enjoys going on raids. He is also a trader, and sells bowls, stolen treasure and slaves at the big trading towns.

Björn, the youngest son, is 19. His name means "bear". He hopes to find land in Iceland to set up his own farm.

FREYDA

COUSIN OLAF

Freyda, Knut's eldest daughter, is 16. Her mother is teaching her to cook, spin and weave. Freyda looks after her two young sisters. There are no schools for them to go to – even Knut cannot read or write.

Olaf, Knut's cousin, is a chieftain too. He owns a big farm and a ship for raiding. People call him Olaf Strongarm, because when he was young, he won many wrestling and weightlifting competitions.

KNUT'S FARM

Your magic time travel helmet has brought you to Knut's farm, which stands on the shores of southern Norway. Winter is over and everyone is busy working on the land. There's a lot to be done.

Knut lives with his family in the main house, called the longhouse. He has slaves and freemen to help him grow food and look after his cows, sheep and horses.

All the slaves live together in a small, stone hut nearby. The freemen live in houses on Knut's land too. Their wives and children help Astrid with the housework and cooking in the longhouse.

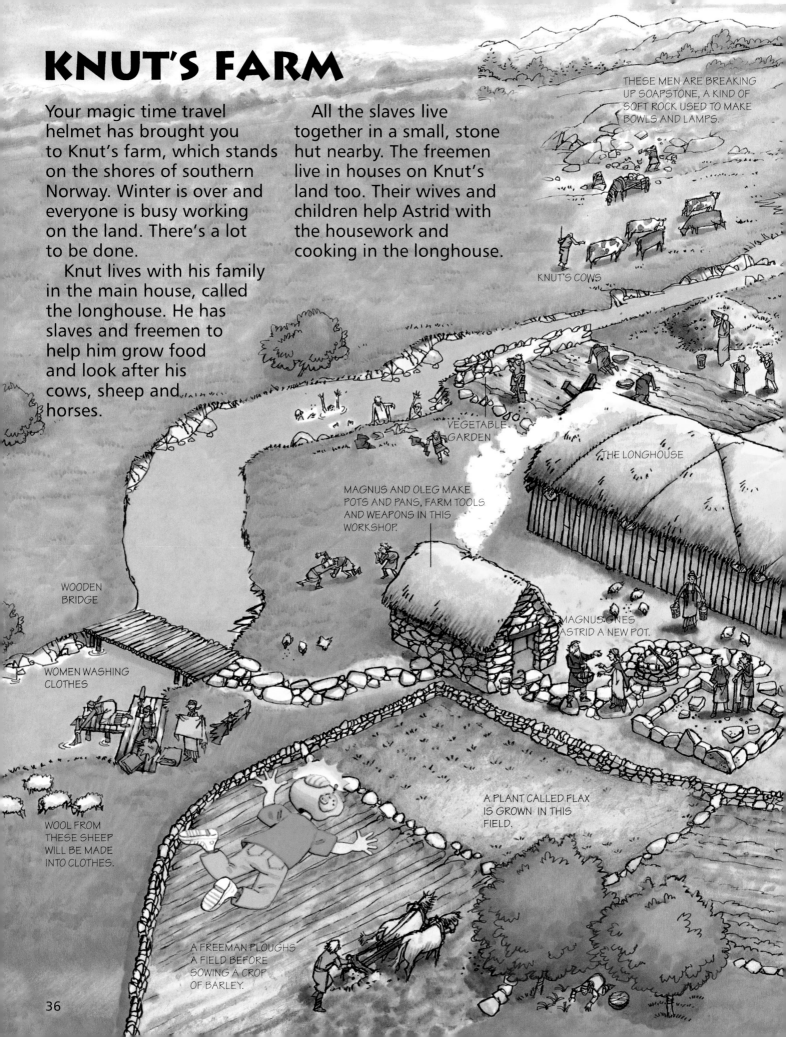

THESE MEN ARE BREAKING UP SOAPSTONE, A KIND OF SOFT ROCK USED TO MAKE BOWLS AND LAMPS.

KNUT'S COWS

VEGETABLE GARDEN

THE LONGHOUSE

MAGNUS AND OLEG MAKE POTS AND PANS, FARM TOOLS AND WEAPONS IN THIS WORKSHOP.

MAGNUS GIVES ASTRID A NEW POT.

WOODEN BRIDGE

WOMEN WASHING CLOTHES

WOOL FROM THESE SHEEP WILL BE MADE INTO CLOTHES.

A PLANT CALLED FLAX IS GROWN IN THIS FIELD.

A FREEMAN PLOUGHS A FIELD BEFORE SOWING A CROP OF BARLEY.

SLAVES DIG UP LUMPS OF METAL CALLED BOG-ORE IN THIS MARSH.

WOOD FOR A NEW SHIP IS COVERED WITH SKINS TO KEEP IT DRY.

CHARCOAL

HALFDAN

BOG-ORE IS MELTED INTO IRON IN FURNACES.

SLAVE HUT

HALFDAN AND TWO FREEMEN ARE HUNTING DEER.

THESE SLAVES ARE CHOPPING WOOD FOR THE FIRE.

ANIMAL HOUSE

CARTS AND SLEDS ARE KEPT DRY IN THIS STORAGE HUT.

KNUT

THIS MAN IS SOWING BARLEY SEEDS.

FOOD IS STORED IN THIS HUT.

THESE YOUNG MEN ARE LEARNING TO FIGHT WITH SWORDS.

SVEN HAS JUST BEEN FISHING. HIS NET IS FULL OF COD AND HERRING.

37

INSIDE KNUT'S LONGHOUSE

This morning, there are lots of people in the longhouse. It has one big room which is always dark, smoky and smelly as there are no windows. There is only a small hole in the roof to let out the smoke from the fire.

Knut is carving arrows. Astrid is weaving cloth for the sail of a new ship and Björn is still asleep in bed.

At one end of the longhouse, some of the women are busy preparing breakfast. Today, the family will eat hot barley and oat porridge, bread, butter, cheese and milk.

MOST PEOPLE SLEEP ON PLATFORMS OR ON THE FLOOR.

KNUT'S AND ASTRID'S BED

BJÖRN

KNUT

SLAVE

MILK

QUERN

FLOUR

MAKING BREAD

HOLE TO PUT IN GRAIN

FLOUR

QUERN

The baker grinds barley in a container called a quern. She turns the handle until the grain has been ground into flour.

KNEADING DOUGH

Next, she mixes the flour with water in a big wooden trough. She kneads them together to make dough.

BAKING THE LOAVES

When the dough is properly mixed, she shapes it into small loaves. She bakes these over the hot ashes of the fire.

MAKING WOOL INTO THREAD

In early summer, Sven uses big metal shears to cut wool off the sheep. Freyda washes the wool in the stream and then hangs it up to dry.

To get rid of any knots, twigs and dirt, Freyda combs the wool with long metal-pronged combs. Then the wool is ready to be spun.

Astrid ties some of the wool to a stick and uses a spindle to pull and twist pieces of wool. Gradually a long, thin thread is formed.

She winds the long thread around a piece of wood called a yarn-winder. Sometimes, she dyes the thread with vegetable juices.

MALLET

HOT PORRIDGE

THIS WOMAN IS BAKING BREAD OVER THE FIRE.

ASTRID IS WEAVING CLOTH TO MAKE A SHIP'S SAIL.

LOOM WEIGHTS

39

BUILDING A NEW WARSHIP

Today, Knut has come to watch his freemen building a new warship. They have been hard at work for many weeks, but now they are nearly finished. The ship, known as a longship, must be strong enough to cross the rough, open sea to Ireland, and there must be enough room for 40 men to live on board.

OLD WARSHIP

BOATHOUSE

CARPENTERS MAKING OARS

THE SHIP IS ABOUT 24M (80FT) LONG AND 5M (16FT) WIDE.

EACH SIDE PLANK OVERLAPS THE ONE BELOW. THIS MAKES THE SHIP STRONGER.

THE LONG, THICK MAST

AT SEA, LITTLE WOODEN DISKS COVER THE OAR HOLES TO STOP WATER GETTING INTO THE SHIP.

STEERING OAR

HOW A SHIP IS BUILT

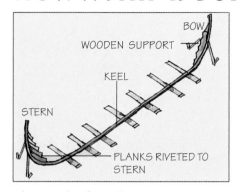

STERN
KEEL
WOODEN SUPPORT
BOW
PLANKS RIVETED TO STERN

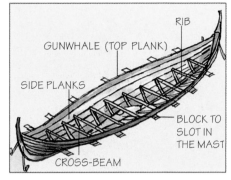

GUNWHALE (TOP PLANK)
RIB
SIDE PLANKS
BLOCK TO SLOT IN THE MAST
CROSS-BEAM

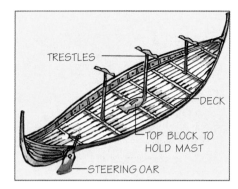

TRESTLES
DECK
TOP BLOCK TO HOLD MAST
STEERING OAR

The trunk of a tall tree is shaped to form the bottom of the boat, called the keel. A curved piece of wood is joined to the front of the keel to make the bow. Another is joined to the back to make the stern.

Planks are attached to the keel, bow and stern to form the bottom and the sides of the ship. Supports called ribs and crossbeams are put inside the ship. A huge block of wood is added to hold up the mast.

Carpenters make a wooden top block to hold the mast. Another piece will be used to keep it upright. Then they make holes for the oars, join a big steering oar, and lay planks to form the deck.

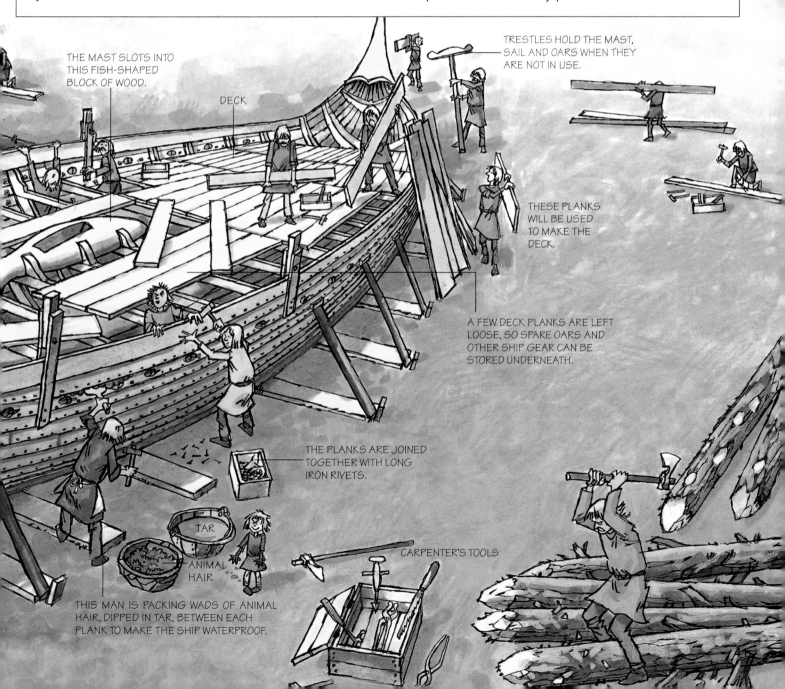

THE MAST SLOTS INTO THIS FISH-SHAPED BLOCK OF WOOD.

DECK

TRESTLES HOLD THE MAST, SAIL AND OARS WHEN THEY ARE NOT IN USE.

THESE PLANKS WILL BE USED TO MAKE THE DECK.

A FEW DECK PLANKS ARE LEFT LOOSE, SO SPARE OARS AND OTHER SHIP GEAR CAN BE STORED UNDERNEATH.

THE PLANKS ARE JOINED TOGETHER WITH LONG IRON RIVETS.

TAR
ANIMAL HAIR

CARPENTER'S TOOLS

THIS MAN IS PACKING WADS OF ANIMAL HAIR, DIPPED IN TAR, BETWEEN EACH PLANK TO MAKE THE SHIP WATERPROOF.

THE RAIDERS GET READY

At last Knut's new ship is finished. Now he can go raiding with his three sons Sven, Halfdan and Björn, and his most trusted freemen. Olaf, Knut's cousin, and two other chieftains have brought their warships and their warriors to join the raiders.

The final preparations are being made before the expedition sets off.

MAGNUS'S WORKSHOP

BATTLE AXES

OLEG

METAL HELMETS

IRON ARROW HEADS

MAGNUS

RAIDERS' SWORDS

SPEARS

CHARCOAL

IRON ORE

TONGS

RIVETS

Magnus the blacksmith is making and mending weapons for the raiders. His assistant, Oleg, keeps the fire glowing with bellows.

When an iron bar is red hot, Magnus removes it from the fire with his tongs and beats it into shape. He is making an axe as a present for Cousin Olaf.

Magnus decorates the swords and axes he makes for chieftains with gold and silver. He can spend as long as a month working on a special weapon.

LEARNING TO FIGHT

THROWING SPEARS

THRUSTING SPEARS

ARCHERS

WRESTLERS

BJÖRN

KNUT IN HIS CHAIN MAIL SHIRT

The Vikings are proud of being good fighters. They own beautiful weapons. Boys learn how to fight when they are very young. Today, Knut and his men are showing off their fighting skills.

Each man has a sword, a spear, an axe and a shield; some have bows and arrows. A few warriors have throwing spears to hurl at enemies, and others have spears specially made for thrusting.

A Viking raider's most precious possession is his sword. It is a sharp and deadly weapon. Only important men, such as Knut and Olaf, own chain mail shirts and metal helmets.

LOADING UP THE SHIP

Everyone is helping to load up the warship with all the equipment and supplies the raiders will need on the voyage to Ireland.

THE RAIDERS SIT ON THEIR SEA CHESTS WHEN THEY ARE ROWING THE SHIP.

OARS

THE RAIDERS DON'T TAKE MUCH FOOD, BECAUSE THEY CAN STEAL MORE FROM THE VILLAGES THEY RAID.

FURS TO KEEP WARM AT NIGHT

FRESH WATER

FREYDA

MILK

BAGS OF DRIED MEAT AND FISH

COOKING EQUIPMENT

COLLAPSIBLE STAND FOR CAULDRON

CARPENTERS' TOOLS

BJÖRN

SHIELD

ASTRID

KNUT

HALFDAN

OIL LAMP

SVEN

COUSIN OLAF

MAGNUS GIVES OLAF A NEW AXE.

SETTING OFF

At dawn, the raiders begin the long, hard voyage to Ireland. It is a good day for sailing. The skies are clear and there's a strong wind.

The raiders will spend several days living and sleeping on their ships. It is very cramped and uncomfortable on board.

Astrid and the other women are sad to see their men go – some will not return. They may be drowned at sea or killed in battle.

THIS MAN IS LOOKING OUT FOR DANGEROUS ROCKS.

THE CREW ARE RAISING THE MAST AND THE SAIL.

STEERING OAR

BY MOVING THE STEERING OAR, OLAF CAN MAKE THE SHIP GO LEFT OR RIGHT.

FREYDA

SVEN

KNUT SAYS GOODBYE TO ASTRID

LIFE ON BOARD

Life on board the ship is very boring. When the weather is calm and the wind is blowing in the right direction, there is nothing to do but eat, sleep and fish. At night, the men sleep on deck in bags made of animal skins. They take turns looking out for land.

THE SQUARE SAIL IS TIED TO A LONG POLE, CALLED THE YARD-ARM, WHICH CAN BE TURNED SO THE SAIL CATCHES THE WIND.

WHILE THE MAST GOES UP, A FEW MEN KEEP THEIR OARS IN THE WATER TO KEEP THE SHIP STEADY.

FINDING THEIR WAY AT SEA

COMPASS

If possible, the Vikings like to sail along coastlines. But when they have to sail out of sight of land, they use the sun, the stars and a kind of compass to help them go in the right direction.

SEALS

OARS

TILLER

HALFDAN

THE MEN ROLL THE SHIP OVER LOGS. THEY PICK UP THE LOGS AT THE BACK AND LAY THEM IN FRONT OF THE SHIP.

SLAVES HELP HALFDAN AND THE CREW PUSH THE SHIP INTO THE WATER.

45

A RAID

Knut and his men have found a monastery in Ireland to raid. The church is full of precious treasures they can steal.

When the people in nearby farms saw the Viking warships arriving, they fled to the monastery hoping its stone walls would protect them. They sent a messenger to get help, so the raiders must attack quickly and leave before help arrives.

NOBLEMAN'S FORT

VIKING WARRIORS RIDE OFF ON STOLEN HORSES TO RAID A NOBLEMAN'S FORT.

A HERDSMAN TRIES TO DRIVE HIS SHEEP AWAY, TO SAVE THEM FROM THE RAIDERS.

YOUNG MONKS RUSH FROM THE SCHOOLHOUSE WHERE THEY HAVE THEIR DAILY LESSONS.

THE CHURCH CONTAINS ALL THE MOST VALUABLE TREASURES.

GOLD CROSS

GOSPEL BOOK

CASKET

KNUT

MONKS

HALFDAN

SVEN

HALFDAN AND SVEN HAVE FOUND A HOARD OF HIDDEN TREASURE.

THESE RAIDERS HAVE BEEN LEFT BEHIND TO GUARD THE SHIPS,

OLAF HAS BEEN WOUNDED BY AN ARROW.

LOCAL HORSEMEN ARE ATTACKING THE VIKINGS. THE VIKINGS LINK THEIR SHIELDS TO DEFEND THEMSELVES.

SOME RAIDERS SLAUGHTER COWS AND SHEEP TO EAT LATER.

A VIKING COUNTS THE PRISONERS. BACK IN NORWAY THEY WILL BE SOLD AS SLAVES.

THE ABBOT

THREE VILLAGERS KILL A VIKING WITH THEIR HUNTING SPEARS.

A MONK'S HOUSE

ONE FAMILY MANAGES TO ESCAPE OVER THE WALL.

47

A FEAST

At the end of the summer, the raiders sailed back to Norway. Their ship was loaded down with loot and prisoners.

Astrid has prepared a huge feast to celebrate their success. For days, the women have worked hard cooking splendid food. Cows and sheep have been slaughtered to roast on spits, and deer and wild boars have been hunted in the forest.

Knut has invited all the local chieftains to the feast. But cousin Olaf has stayed at home. He was wounded during a raid and is gravely ill.

Everyone wears their best clothes for the feast. The longhouse rings with their laughter and songs. The raiders tell stories of terrible storms at sea, and the strange lands and people they have seen.

HORN

BEER

WILD BOAR STEAKS COOK ON THE FIRE

SLICES OF BEEF

ROAST SHEEP

EVERYONE GETS VERY DIRTY EATING WITH THEIR FINGERS.

GAMING BOARD

KNUT'S GIFTS TO ASTRID

SILVER NECKLACE

GLASS BEADS

GOLD BRACELETS

RINGS

SHAWL BROOCHES

NECKLACE

BRONZE BROOCHES

Magnus, the blacksmith, has been very busy since the raiders returned. He has made many fine brooches, necklaces, rings and bracelets for Astrid.

They are made from gold coins and silver bowls which have been melted down. Knut has also stolen many jewels on his raids and has given them to Astrid to wear.

ASTRID'S CASKET

RUNES

This is Astrid's new jewel box. The words "Astrid a Kistu Thasa", which means "Astrid owns this casket", have been carved on it in Viking letters, known as runes.

THE GUESTS DRINK FROM COWS' HORNS, GLASSES AND WOODEN CUPS.

A POET RECITES POEMS WHICH TELL OF BRAVE DEEDS AND GREAT BATTLES.

A CHIEFTAIN TOASTS KNUT AND ASTRID.

THE CHIEFTAINS DRINK WINE FROM FRANCE. EVERYONE ELSE DRINKS ASTRID'S SPECIALLY BREWED BEER.

VEAL STEW

KNUT

WINE

ASTRID

BOWLS OF HERBS

SVEN

FREDYA GREETS THE MAN SHE IS GOING TO MARRY.

PEAS

MAGNUS

CABBAGE

A SLAVE SERVES A LEG OF DEER.

THIS MAN IS CARVING ASTRID'S NAME ON A STOLEN CASKET.

COOKING MEAT

HOT STONES

MEAT

WOOD-LINED PIT

HOT STONES

Some meat is roasted on a spit. This is a long, iron rod which can be turned with a handle. The head and feet of the dead animal are cut off first.

Sometimes meat is baked in a big hole in the ground. Hot stones are packed around the meat, and it is covered with soil until it is cooked.

Another way of cooking meat is to boil it. A wood-lined pit is filled with water, and chunks of meat are put into it. To make the meat more tasty, the cook adds herbs, such as cumin, juniper berries, mustard seeds and garlic. Then he drops hot stones from the fire into the pit to heat up the water.

COUSIN OLAF DIES

Olaf is in bed. The wounds he received while raiding have made him very ill. A doctor is trying to save his life with medicine made from herbs.

Knut and Astrid pray to the Viking gods. They believe that the gods are fearless warriors, who can perform magical deeds.

They beg Thor, who is the god of thunder, and Odin, the chief of the gods, to answer their prayers and save Olaf's life.

OLAF HAS A CHARM, KNOWN AS AN AMULET, TO KEEP EVIL SPIRITS AWAY. IT IS SHAPED LIKE THE HAMMER THAT THE GOD THOR IS BELIEVED TO CARRY.

OLAF'S WIFE

THESE WOMEN ARE PRAYING TO A STATUE OF THOR. THEY OFFER IT GIFTS OF WINE AND FOOD.

ASTRID

KNUT

HOT WATER

DOCTOR CHANGING THE BANDAGES

OLAF'S HUNTING DOG

THE DOCTOR HAS MADE A MEDICINE FROM HERBS.

BURIAL PREPARATIONS

Unfortunately, medicine and prayers didn't save Olaf's life. His wife prepares his body for burial. He will be buried in his best clothes.

Olaf's body is carried to the family cemetery in a horse-drawn wagon. His father and his mother are already buried there.

Olaf's finest horses and his faithful hunting dog are led away to be killed. They will be buried with Olaf in his grave.

THE BURIAL

Cousin Olaf was a famous and wealthy man, so he is buried with his warship. A special wooden chamber has been built on the deck for his body to lie in. The Vikings believe people have another life after they die. They think Olaf will sail to the next world in his ship.

His possessions are buried with him so he can use them in his next life.

SOIL TO FILL IN THE GRAVE

THE GRAVE OF OLAF'S MOTHER

THE GRAVE OF OLAF'S FATHER

HOW OTHER VIKINGS ARE BURIED

Poor people are usually buried in a big hole with a few of their belongings. This woman has been buried with two spindles, a comb and a barrel of milk.

Dead warriors are often burned on a pile of wood, called a pyre. Their swords are bent, their spears broken, and their shields slashed and thrown on the fire.

Occasionally slaves are killed and buried with their masters, so they can carry on serving in the next life. This man was a rich farmer, so he has a wood-lined grave.

51

BJÖRN SAILS TO ICELAND

Knut's son Björn has decided to take his family to live in Iceland. There isn't enough good land left in Norway for him to farm.

It will take him several weeks to get to Iceland. He will sail in a new ship his father has given him. It is big enough to hold a lot

of cargo. Some freemen and a few slaves are going with Björn. They will help him build a farmhouse and work on the land.

1 GETTING READY TO LEAVE

BJÖRN

WEAVING LOOM

COWS FOR BREEDING

SLED

MILK AND FRESH WATER

The settlers are loading the ship with bags of barley seed to plant on the farm and animals to breed. They are also taking household things and camping gear.

2 VISITING THE SHETLAND ISLANDS

On the way to Iceland, Björn visits some people who have a farm on one of the tiny Shetland Islands.

BJÖRN'S SHIP

SHETLAND PONIES

3 SHIPWRECKED ON THE FAROES

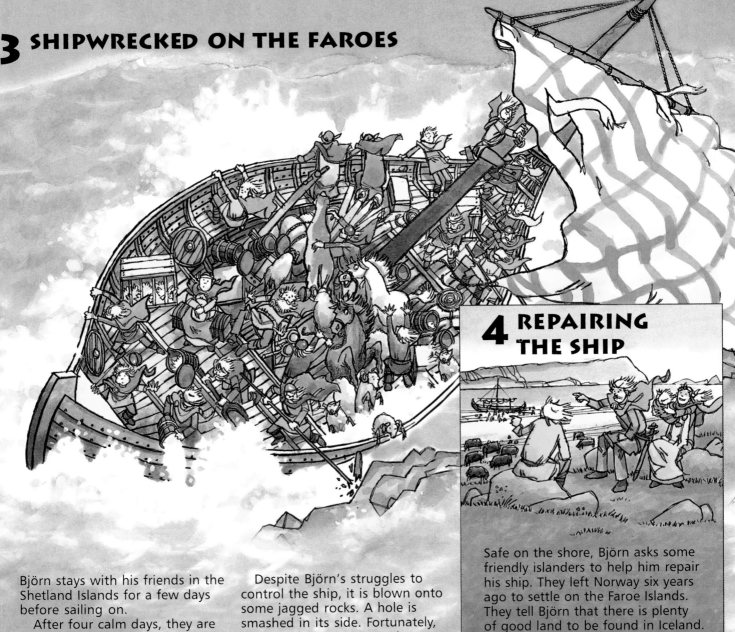

Björn stays with his friends in the Shetland Islands for a few days before sailing on.

After four calm days, they are caught in a bad storm near the coast of the Faroe Islands.

Despite Björn's struggles to control the ship, it is blown onto some jagged rocks. A hole is smashed in its side. Fortunately, the crew manage to row it to the shore.

4 REPAIRING THE SHIP

Safe on the shore, Björn asks some friendly islanders to help him repair his ship. They left Norway six years ago to settle on the Faroe Islands. They tell Björn that there is plenty of good land to be found in Iceland.

5 ARRIVING IN ICELAND

When the ship is ready, Björn sets off once again. After many days at sea, he sees Iceland on the horizon. It is a strange island, with plumes of smoke and steam from volcanoes, and jagged, treeless mountains topped with snow.

Björn finds that there are already people living on the flat land on the south coast of the island. But further west, he discovers some unclaimed land that looks good for farming.

VOLCANO

SEALS

BJÖRN'S LAND

GLACIER

FISHERMEN

SETTLED LAND

53

SVEN GOES TRADING

Hedeby is a large trading town in Norway. It is a very exciting place, full of Viking merchants busy exchanging their goods.

Today, Sven has brought his share of the loot from the winter raids to trade. He has six slaves, a bag of silver, and some bowls to sell. He wants to exchange them for silk cloth and exotic things from foreign countries.

Arab merchants have come overland from Asia to sell silk and buy slaves. Some of the Viking women can't help staring at their unusual clothes.

In Hedeby, there are many craftsmen hard at work, making combs, leather shoes and cloth to trade. There are clay pots, amber beads, farm tools, ropes and weapons on sale as well.

THIS FENCE PROTECTS THE SHIPS.

HOUSES MADE OF SPLIT LOGS

TRADING SHIPS

FISH

A GUARD KEEPS WATCH FOR INVADERS.

A WALL OF SOIL AND WOOD TO STOP INVADERS

SVEN BUYS SILK AND WINE

ARAB TRADER SELLING SILK

SOAPSTONE BOWLS

SVEN

BARRELS OF WINE

In a few days time, there will be a festival at Knut's farm. Sven buys wine and drinking glasses for the feast. In exchange, he gives three slaves and some silver arm bands.

The silver is weighed on scales to find out how much it is worth.

Later on, Sven is planning to sell three more slaves and some bowls to buy silk for his wife.

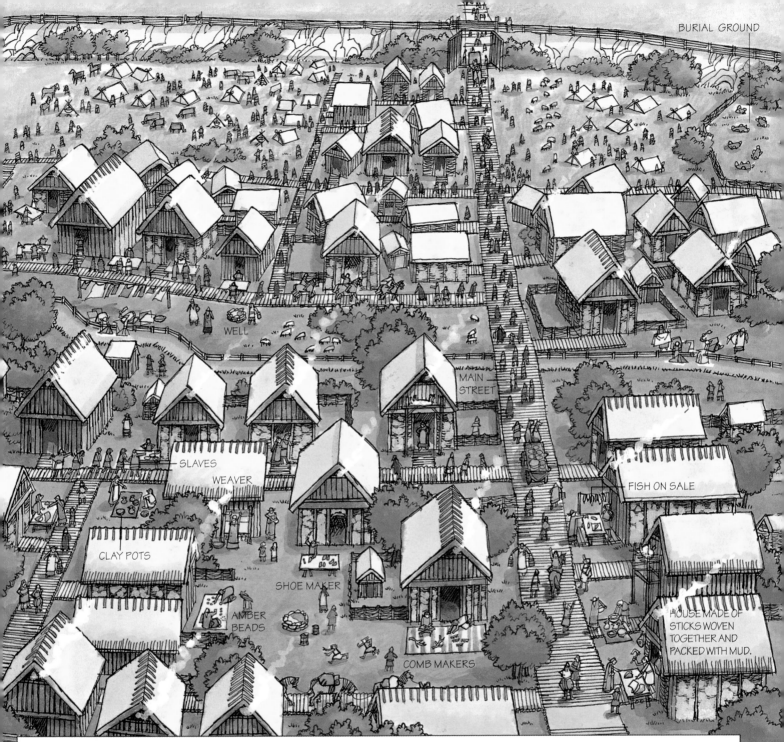

BURIAL GROUND

WELL

MAIN STREET

SLAVES

WEAVER

FISH ON SALE

CLAY POTS

SHOE MAKER

AMBER BEADS

COMB MAKERS

HOUSE MADE OF STICKS WOVEN TOGETHER AND PACKED WITH MUD.

MAKING COMBS

ANTLER

This craftsman is making combs out of a deer's antler. He cuts the points off the antler and shaves down the rough outside.

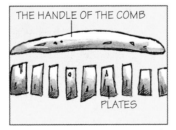

THE HANDLE OF THE COMB

PLATES

Then, he carves a smooth, flat strip to make the handle of the comb. He cuts lots of small plates which will make the teeth.

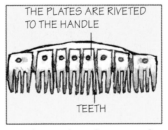

THE PLATES ARE RIVETED TO THE HANDLE

TEETH

He rivets the plates to the handle, and then cuts them into fine teeth. Finally, he decorates the comb with carvings.

COMB CASES

SPOONS

Craftsmen also make comb cases, spoons and handles for knives out of bone. They sell them to traders who come to town.

55

BJÖRN SETTLES IN ICELAND

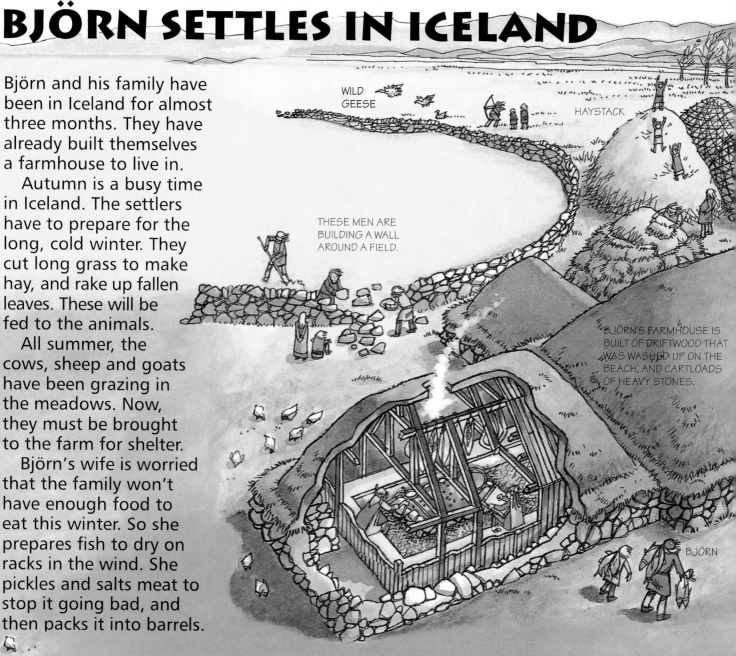

Björn and his family have been in Iceland for almost three months. They have already built themselves a farmhouse to live in.

Autumn is a busy time in Iceland. The settlers have to prepare for the long, cold winter. They cut long grass to make hay, and rake up fallen leaves. These will be fed to the animals.

All summer, the cows, sheep and goats have been grazing in the meadows. Now, they must be brought to the farm for shelter.

Björn's wife is worried that the family won't have enough food to eat this winter. So she prepares fish to dry on racks in the wind. She pickles and salts meat to stop it going bad, and then packs it into barrels.

WILD GEESE

HAYSTACK

THESE MEN ARE BUILDING A WALL AROUND A FIELD.

BJÖRN'S FARMHOUSE IS BUILT OF DRIFTWOOD THAT WAS WASHED UP ON THE BEACH, AND CARTLOADS OF HEAVY STONES.

BJÖRN

WORK IN ICELAND

CAULDRONS OF SEAWATER

The settlers need salt to preserve their meat. So they fill big cauldrons with seawater and seaweed, and heat them over a fire. When all the water has boiled away, crystals of salt are left in the bottom of the pots.

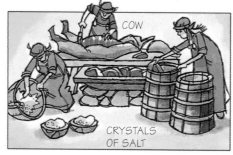

COW

CRYSTALS OF SALT

One woman scrapes the crystals from the pots, while another chops up a dead cow. Strips of the meat are packed in barrels with the salt. This preserves the meat, stopping it from going bad.

Björn's wife dries chunks of meat and cod over a fire. A freeman teaches his son how to light a fire made of moss and twigs. He strikes a hard stone against a piece of iron to make the first sparks.

COLLECTING GRASS

THE ANIMALS ARE LED TO SHELTER.

THICK BLOCKS OF TURF COVER THE ROOF OF THE FARMHOUSE TO KEEP OUT THE COLD.

ANIMAL BARN

BJÖRN'S WIFE

GUTTED FISH

RACKS OF COD AND HERRING

NETTING BIRDS

During the spring in Iceland, thousands of guillemots and puffins nest on the cliffs. Men climb up and trap the birds in nets. These men have caught many birds to eat.

Whale meat is good to eat, and the blubber can be melted down to use in oil lamps. Björn and his crew often hunt whales. When they spot one, they drive it into shallow water and kill it with their spears.

The settlers also eat seal meat, and use sealskins to make ropes and shoes. These hunters have found some seals basking in the sun. They will spear as many as they can before the seals slip back into the sea.

These women are collecting downy feathers from eider ducks' nests. They will use them to fill pillows and bed covers. If the ducks have left their eggs in the nests, the women take these too.

A MEETING OF THE *THING*

Knut and other freemen from this area of Norway have come to a big meeting. It is called the *Thing*, and is held a few times a year.

Today they discuss important local business matters, and decide how to punish three criminals. Some women join in the discussions.

People set up their tents, because the *Thing* will last for many days. There will be plenty of time for games, gossip and trading.

THIS WOMAN HAS BEEN FOUND GUILTY OF BEING A WITCH. SHE WILL BE DROWNED.

THIS MAN IS A THIEF. HE WILL HAVE ONE HAND CUT OFF.

OLEG

LAW SPEAKER

KNUT

Oleg has been accused of murdering his master, Magnus the blacksmith. Today everyone will hear evidence about the killing.

But Oleg refuses to answer questions. A man chosen to be the law speaker reminds the crowd of the law. They must all agree on Oleg's punishment.

The crowd find Oleg guilty of murder. He is forced to leave Norway forever. He must go quickly before one of Magnus's family kills him.

WEIGHTLIFTING

Vikings love to show off their strength. Some men have been lifting huge boulders to see who can pick up the heaviest. This man has won.

WRESTLING

Wrestling is also popular. The toughest Vikings compete against each other to see who is the best and strongest wrestler.

STALLION FIGHTING

Fierce, wild stallions are specially bred for fighting. Sometimes, during a fight, the horses' owners get excited, and start to fight each other too.

A FESTIVAL

Knut and Astrid have invited their family and friends to a festival at the farm tonight.

Astrid and Freyda are preparing the food and drink, and Sven is collecting firewood. Halfdan has been hunting. He killed some deer and rabbits, which will be eaten at the feast.

Everyone is very excited, because feasts are great fun. There will be lots of eating and drinking, while poets and singers entertain the guests.

SVEN

WOOD FOR THE FIRE

STORE HOUSE

ASTRID

KNUT

DRIED MEAT AND FISH

FREYDA

SPECIALLY BREWED BEER

A SLAVE HAS CLEARED THE SNOW OFF THE ICE.

DEER

HALFDAN

WOODEN SKIS

BONE SKATES

59

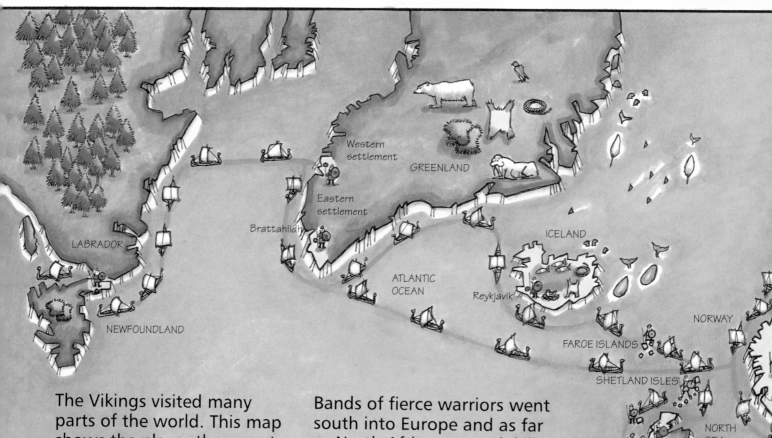

Western settlement

GREENLAND

Eastern settlement

Brattahlidh

LABRADOR

ATLANTIC OCEAN

ICELAND

Reykjavik

NEWFOUNDLAND

NORWAY

FAROE ISLANDS

SHETLAND ISLES

NORTH SEA

IRELAND

York

Dublin

BRITAIN

London

Rouen
Paris
R. SEINE

Nantes

R. LOIRE

FRANCE
Bordeaux

Santiago

SPAIN

Lisbon

Cordoba

Seville

The Vikings visited many parts of the world. This map shows the places they went to, the routes they took, the people they met, and the things they found.

They raided and settled in towns in Britain and Ireland.

Bands of fierce warriors went south into Europe and as far as North Africa, to steal, kill and trade. In Central Asia, they met Arabs to trade with.

Some Vikings sailed west to explore and settle in Iceland, Greenland and North America.

WHAT THE VIKINGS FOUND

TIMBER	WEAPONS	JEWELS
FURS	FEATHERS	WHEAT
WALRUS IVORY	SOAP-STONE	TIN
HIDES	CLOTH	HONEY
ROPES	SLAVES	SALT
FISH	LOOT	WINE

POTTERY	FALCONS	ARABS
GLASS	SPICES	SLAVS
GOLD	SWORD BLADES	VIKINGS
AMBER	VIKING OVERLAND ROUTES	FRANKS
SILVER	VIKING RIVER ROUTES	CARAVAN ROUTES
SILK	VIKING SEA ROUTES	TRADING TOWNS

ARCTIC
OCEAN

Staraja
Lagoda

Novgorod

Birka

SWEDEN

Grobina

Wiskiauten

Truso

Wolin

R. ELBE

Cracow

Prague

nz

R. DANUBE

Rome

ITALY

SARDINIA

SICILY

MEDITERRANEAN SEA

NORTH AFRICA

Bulgar

Kiev

R. DNEIPER

BLACK SEA

Constantinople

CRETE

CYPRUS

Sidon

Jerusalem

Alexandria

R. VOLGA

ARAL
SEA

CASPIAN SEA

Tashkent

Samarkand

Bokhara

Gurgan

R. TIGRIS

R. EUPHRATES

Baghdad

PERSIAN
GULF

THE STORY OF THE VIKINGS

The first Viking raids began in about 793. A band of warriors attacked a monastery off Lindisfarne, a small island on the northeast coast of Britain. They murdered many people and took others as slaves. News of this attack spread terror all over Europe.

RAIDING A VILLAGE

A year later, raiders attacked monasteries at Monkwearmouth and Jarrow, in northern England. In 795, Vikings from Norway began raiding Ireland, killing and looting. A few of them settled on the Scottish islands, and the Isle of Man.

VIKING SETTLERS

Other Viking raiders sailed along the coasts of France, Germany, Spain, Italy and North Africa. There, they stole whatever riches they could find.

RAIDERS WITH LOOT

Swedish Vikings went east to Russia, sailing down the Volga and Dneiper rivers to raid and settle in towns such as Staraja Ladoga, Kiev, Novgorod and Gnezdovo.

SAILING THE GREAT RIVERS

The Vikings believed in their own gods, such as Thor, Odin and Frey. In 830, a missionary monk went to Birka, in Sweden, to convert people to Christianity. But he didn't have much success.

A MONK PREACHING

After 835, the raids on England and Ireland became more and more frequent. Vikings began to set up camps, where they rested over winter. Then they began raiding again in the spring. In 841, they settled in Ireland for the first time.

A WINTER CAMP

Many Vikings began to settle in other countries. In 860, Norwegian explorers discovered Iceland. Farmers settled there ten years later. By 930, about 10,000 Vikings were living there. A parliament was set up in Iceland, called the *Althing*.

THE ALTHING

In 867, Danish Vikings in England captured York and settled all over Northumbria. After many battles between the Danes and the English, a treaty was signed between them. It divided the country between them. The Danish part was called the Danelaw.

SIGNING THE TREATY

This treaty didn't bring peace. The Vikings continued their raids. It wasn't until 926, when Aethelstan was King of England, that the English managed to recapture Northumbria from the Danes. Aethelstan gathered a huge army and defeated the Danes in battle.

AETHELSTAN DEFEATS THE DANES

Early in the 10th century, bands of Vikings sailed from Ireland, attacking northwest England. Many Vikings began to settle in northern Scotland. In Ireland, Dublin and Limerick became important trading ports.

DUBLIN

In 911, Rollo, a Danish chieftain, took his warriors to Normandy in France. They captured land from the Franks. Their leader, Charles the Simple, signed a treaty with Rollo, which made Normandy Viking territory.

ROLLO AND CHARLES

In about 930, the Danish Vikings started to become Christians. Their king, Harald Bluetooth, was converted ten years later. In Norway, people were forced by their king to adopt Christianity, but many continued to worship their own Viking gods.

THE VIKINGS ARE CONVERTED.

In 982, Eric the Red, a Viking who had been banished from Norway for killing a man, heard of an unexplored island. He went to live on this island, which he called Greenland. Later, he persuaded many other people to live there with him.

ERIC THE RED ON GREENLAND

In 1002, Eric's son, Leif Ericsson, sailed west from Greenland, and found an island which he called Vinland. This was probably Newfoundland. Some Vikings followed Leif to live there.

LEIF SEES VINLAND.

Early in the 11th century, the English were forced to pay money to the Vikings to leave their towns and people in peace. The money, called Danegeld, was paid for several years. But the Vikings kept returning – until 1016, when King Canute of Denmark invaded, and became the King of England.

PAYING THE DANEGELD

In the early 11th century, the Norwegian Vikings became Christians. They built churches and set up stones, called rune stones, in memory of people who had died. But it was not until the 12th century that the Swedish Vikings finally became Christians.

RUNE STONES AND A CHURCH

Christianity began to change the Vikings' way of life. They weren't so fierce and no longer went on many raids. By 1066, the raids ceased and the Vikings settled down to a quieter life. But they were still great traders all over Europe.

THE VIKINGS SETTLE DOWN.

Wherever the Vikings settled, they adopted the language and customs of the local people. They soon became French, English, Irish, Russian, or Scots themselves.

Later, the people in Scandinavia became known as Norwegians, Swedes and Danes. Even today, in the countries in which they settled, you can see the descendants of the tall, blond and blue-eyed Vikings.

VIKING RAIDERS
TIME QUIZ

1. What is the name given to the big house that Knut and his family live in?
2. A quern is used by the baker in Knut's longhouse. What is it?
3. What do the Viking raiders sit on when they are rowing their warship?
4. What can you see Knut stealing from the monastery in Ireland?
5. What are Viking letters known as?
6. Who is Thor?
7. What is the name of the trading town in Norway that Sven visits?
8. What is a *Thing*?
9. What did Halfdan bring home from his hunting trip for the family to eat at the festival?
10. What name is given to the carved stones that Vikings erect in memory of people who have died?

Answers on page 130.

NEXT STOP
ROME & ROMANS

Contents

BACK TO ANCIENT ROME

Your third journey will take you from Knut's settlement in northern Europe, to Rome during the time of the Romans. You will arrive in Italy in the year 100.

To make this journey, you need to travel back nearly 800 years, so you will need to use your magic helmet.

In museums you'll find pieces of Roman furniture, and see pictures of Roman people at work or play. But museums can't show you everything you want to see. This visit will enable you to see exactly what everyday life was like in Roman times. You will meet a Roman family, visit a beautiful bath-house, see gladiators fighting in an arena, and march into battle to defend part of the Roman empire.

1. SET YOUR TIME HELMET

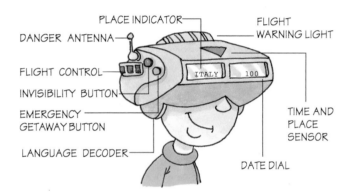

PLACE INDICATOR
DANGER ANTENNA
FLIGHT CONTROL
INVISIBILITY BUTTON
EMERGENCY GETAWAY BUTTON
LANGUAGE DECODER
FLIGHT WARNING LIGHT
ITALY   100
TIME AND PLACE SENSOR
DATE DIAL

Before you begin your third journey through time, make sure that you remember to change the Date Dial and Place Indicator on your magic time travel helmet.

Set the date to "100", and the place to "Italy".

2. YOUR DESTINATION

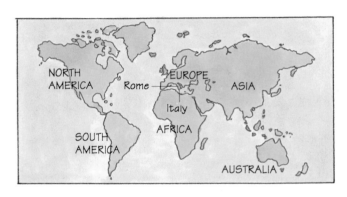

NORTH AMERICA   EUROPE   ASIA
Rome
Italy
SOUTH AMERICA   AFRICA
AUSTRALIA

Your new destination is Rome. Rome is the main city in the area of southern Europe now known as Italy.

Below you can see the Viking settlement you are leaving and the Roman house you will arrive at.

3. GO!

890

You are hovering above the bleak shores of Greenland. Björn and his family are busy building their new settlement before the winter comes. One moment you are watching them gather wood and stones, the next you are off on a journey that will take you back nearly 800 years.

100

With your magic helmet flashing, you fly through time and space. In just a few seconds you arrive in Roman times. Everything around you has changed. The family in this house are sitting beside a charcoal stove. They are dressed in loose robes.

THE PEOPLE YOU WILL MEET

Everyone you will meet on this trip lives in the city of Rome, which is in the country now called Italy.

Most of the people who live in and around Rome are known as Romans. Only slaves and foreign visitors are not called Romans.

You will come across both rich and poor people, and you will be able to see how different their lives are.

Roman men are called citizens. There are three main types of citizens: noblemen, businessmen and ordinary people, such as farmers, storekeepers and craftsmen.

Poor storekeepers and craftsmen are often men who have been set free from slavery by their masters.

Wealthy people have pleasant, easy lives, because they have lots of slaves to do all the work.

Slaves are mostly captured foreigners, who are bought at slave markets. If they run away, they are beaten or put to death.

PETRONIUS AND HIS FAMILY

The main people you will meet are a nobleman named Petronius, his wife, Livia, and their family.

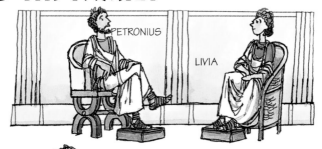

Petronius is a rich man who lives in a large house in Rome. He is a lawyer and an important official in the government. Livia looks after the house, and has many slaves to help her.

MARCUS

Marcus is 16 and training to be a soldier. Like all children, he has to obey his father and ask permission before he does anything.

CORNELIA

Cornelia is the eldest daughter. She is 14 years old and engaged to a young nobleman. Until her wedding, she will live at home.

MARIUS

Marius is 15 years old. He is learning about his father's business. When he is older, he will serve in the army for a while, like Marcus.

CLAUDIA

Claudia is 12 and lives at home. She has finished school. Now her mother is teaching her to spin and weave. A tutor gives her music lessons.

CAIUS

Caius, the youngest, is eight and goes to school. He doesn't like the schoolmaster and would rather play all day.

AUNT ANTONIA

Petronius's sister Antonia and her children live with the family. Her husband was killed while he was fighting with the army.

SESTIUS

Sestius is Petronius's cousin. He is visiting the family to ask for Petronius's help with some legal business.

PERICLES

Pericles is Petronius's secretary. He used to be a slave, but he works so well that Petronius has given him his freedom.

THE ROAD TO ROME

The year is AD100, and your time travel helmet has brought you to Italy. You are hovering above a road just outside Rome.

Rome is the biggest city in Europe. Only 700 years before your visit, it was just a village of wooden huts built on one of seven hills. Gradually, the city grew and now there are stone houses, temples and public buildings built on all of the seven hills.

Today, there are lots of people on the road to Rome.

HUNTERS ARE COOKING A WILD BOAR OVER A FIRE.

THIS IS A TAVERN WHERE PEOPLE CAN BUY FOOD AND GET A BED FOR THE NIGHT.

TOMBSTONES

A MESSENGER CARRYING A LETTER TO ROME

MILESTONES MARK THE DISTANCE TO THE MIDDLE OF ROME.

ROAD MENDERS

SESTIUS IS GOING TO STAY WITH HIS COUSIN PETRONIUS.

A PAVED ROAD FOR FAST TRAFFIC AND IMPORTANT PEOPLE

THE MUDDY TRACKS ARE FOR FARM CARTS AND POOR PEOPLE.

TOMBSTONES – NO ONE IS ALLOWED TO BE BURIED INSIDE ROME.

A STAGING POST WHERE MESSENGERS CAN LEAVE TIRED HORSES AND MOUNT FRESH ONES

THIS PIPELINE, CALLED AN AQUEDUCT, CARRIES FRESH WATER TO ROME.

THE CITY OF ROME

FRUIT TREES

CARTS CARRY FRESH FOOD TO THE CITY.

BARGES CARRY GRAIN FROM AFRICA AND EGYPT INTO ROME.

THIS FARMER IS PLOUGHING HIS FIELD BEFORE SOWING A SPRING CROP

THE TIBER RIVER

FISHERMEN

69

IN THE STREETS OF ROME

The Romans rule over an empire which is made up of the many lands they have conquered. Rome is the capital of this empire.

It is a splendid city, with huge palaces, beautiful houses, bathhouses and arches. Many of the finest buildings shine in the sun because they are covered with thin slabs of marble.

At the time of your journey, the Romans are so powerful that Rome doesn't need walls to protect it from enemies.

In the middle of the city are several open squares called forums. They were built at different times by different Roman emperors.

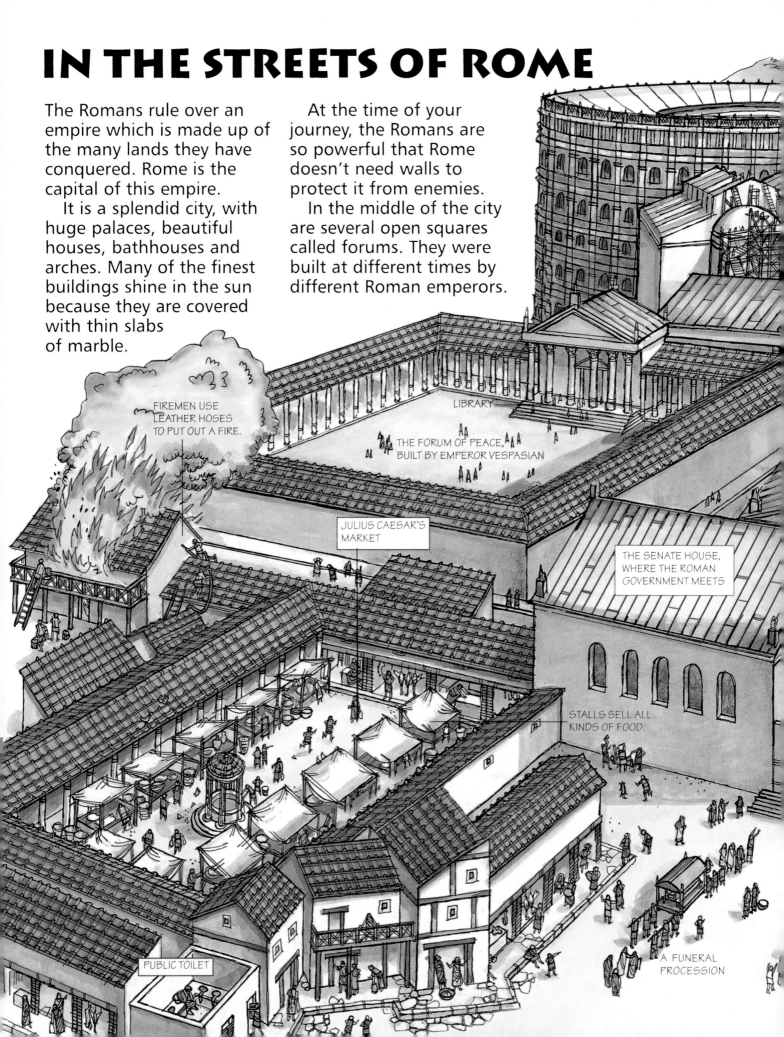

FIREMEN USE LEATHER HOSES TO PUT OUT A FIRE.

LIBRARY

THE FORUM OF PEACE, BUILT BY EMPEROR VESPASIAN

JULIUS CAESAR'S MARKET

THE SENATE HOUSE, WHERE THE ROMAN GOVERNMENT MEETS

STALLS SELL ALL KINDS OF FOOD.

PUBLIC TOILET

A FUNERAL PROCESSION

A HUGE ARENA
CALLED THE COLOSSEUM

THE PALACE WHERE THE
ROMAN EMPEROR LIVES

THE BASILICA
AEMILIA,
WHERE MEN DO
BUSINESS

TEMPLE OF THE VESTALS,
WHERE PRIESTESSES
KEEP A FIRE BURNING
ALL THE TIME

TEMPLE
OF CAESAR

THESE SOLDIERS ARE MARCHING
THROUGH THE CITY TO CELEBRATE
WINNING A BATTLE.

A THIEF

THIS PLATFORM IS CALLED
THE NEW ROSTRA. IT IS USED
BY PUBLIC SPEAKERS.

PETRONIUS AT HOME

This is where Petronius lives. He has a very large and comfortable house because he is wealthy and important.

The house has high walls and small windows to prevent thieves from getting in. The floors are made of stone. In the middle of the house there is a large hall which has an open roof.

Petronius is the master of his household and everyone has to obey him. But he is kind, and treats his slaves and servants well. When he wants new slaves, he buys them at a slave market.

This morning, Petronius is busy working in his office with his secretary, Pericles. A man has come to ask if he can borrow a large sum of money. Marius watches his father doing business.

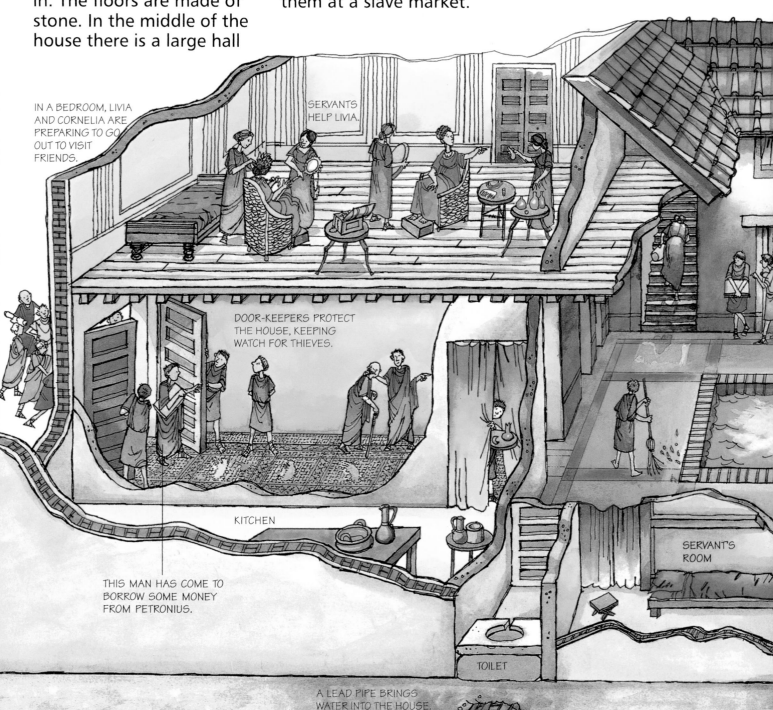

IN A BEDROOM, LIVIA AND CORNELIA ARE PREPARING TO GO OUT TO VISIT FRIENDS.

SERVANTS HELP LIVIA.

DOOR-KEEPERS PROTECT THE HOUSE, KEEPING WATCH FOR THIEVES.

KITCHEN

THIS MAN HAS COME TO BORROW SOME MONEY FROM PETRONIUS.

SERVANT'S ROOM

TOILET

A LEAD PIPE BRINGS WATER INTO THE HOUSE.

A DRAIN CARRIES AWAY DIRTY WATER.

Petronius sees important visitors at once. Less important people often have to wait in the street.

When his business is done, Petronius may visit friends, or go to the law courts to take care of legal matters.

PUTTING ON A TOGA

Before he sees visitors, Petronius puts on a robe which is known as a toga. A slave carefully arranges the folds of heavy material for him.

Only men who are citizens of Rome are allowed to wear togas.

TOGA

A SLAVE BRINGS SESTIUS WARM WATER TO WASH IN.

SESTIUS WAKES UP AFTER HIS LONG, TIRING JOURNEY TO ROME.

ALTAR – WHERE THE FAMILY PRAYS

DINING ROOM

PERICLES KEEPS THE ACCOUNT BOOKS.

PETRONIUS

RAIN WATER COLLECTS IN THIS POOL.

CHARCOAL STOVE

MARIUS IS LEARNING ABOUT HIS FATHER'S BUSINESS.

SLAVES ARE PICKING UP DEAD LEAVES.

THE CHILDREN ARE EATING BREAKFAST, WATCHED BY AUNT ANTONIA.

GOING TO SCHOOL

Caius is on his way to school. Lessons begin so early in the morning that it is still dark, and Caius carries a torch to light his way.

Roman families pay schoolmasters to teach their children. The children of very wealthy families are taught at home by tutors.

Sometimes tutors who are set free from slavery start up their own schools.

FAMILIES LIVE IN THE ROOMS ABOVE THE STORES AND SCHOOLS.

A BAKER GETS UP EARLY TO SELL BREAD TO THE CHILDREN.

CAIUS LIGHTS HIS WAY TO SCHOOL WITH A TORCH.

OIL LAMP

A FAMOUS WRITER

THIS BOY FORGOT HIS LESSON.

THIS SLAVE IS TAKING A BOY TO SCHOOL.

OLDER BOYS LEARN GREEK AND LATIN, GEOMETRY AND HISTORY.

GAMES

School finishes early in the afternoon, so there is plenty of time for the children to play games.

HOOPS ARE FUN FOR ROLLING AND JUMPING THROUGH.

WOODEN SWORDS

THESE GIRLS ARE PLAYING A GAME CALLED JACKS, WITH FIVE SMALL BONES AND A BALL.

STICK AND BALL GAMES

WRITING

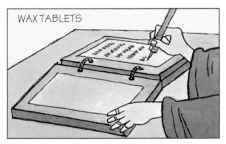

Schoolchildren write on boards spread with wax. They scratch words or sums in the wax with pointed sticks. They can erase mistakes with the flat end of the stick.

Roman books are rolls of paper, called scrolls. They are written by hand. Each end of the roll is stuck to a rod. Readers have to unroll the paper to see each page.

People write on scrolls with pens made of small reeds or of copper. They use ink made from a mixture of soot, a kind of tar called pitch, and black ink from an octopus.

A FAMOUS THINKER

SCHOOL-MASTER

A NAUGHTY BOY DRAWING ON A WALL.

A BOY RECITING A POEM HE HAS LEARNED.

THIS IS A SCHOOL FOR YOUNG CHILDREN. THEY LEARN TO READ AND WRITE AND DO SIMPLE MATHEMATICS.

JAVELINS

CHILDREN LEARN TO SWIM WITH BAMBOO FLOATS.

FLOAT

BOYS RACING THEIR CARTS PRETEND TO BE REAL CHARIOTEERS.

GOING SHOPPING

Petronius and Livia have gone shopping in Rome's narrow, dusty streets. There are weavers, silversmiths and shoemakers. At the bakery below, people are baking bread for the customers.

Rich people only go shopping for their clothes, jewels and other expensive things. They send their servants or slaves to buy food and wine.

Every day, fresh food is sold in the city at open-air markets. Very early in the morning, noisy wooden carts bring the goods into Rome from farms outside.

WHEAT

STONE MILL

FLOUR

LOAVES IN THE OVEN

DOUGH

AT THE BAKERY, WHEAT IS GROUND INTO FLOUR. IT IS MIXED INTO DOUGH, AND BAKED IN THE OVEN.

CUSTOMERS

People stop in the streets to gossip and hear the latest news of the wars and the empire.

Livia and Petronius are buying material from a cloth merchant. Livia wants a new tunic to wear at a feast.

A pharmacist makes ointments from herbs, flowers and seeds. People who are sick also buy magic spells.

CLEANING CLOTHES

Rich Romans have their togas cleaned by men called fullers. The togas are spread on frames and bleached white.

Then the fullers put the togas in tubs of water and a special clay. They tread on them to get all the dirt out.

The clothes are dried and folded, and then put in a big press to flatten them. The Romans do not have irons.

Slaves collect their masters' clean clothes. They have to make sure the work has been done well before paying.

THE MARKET

Today is a market day. Stalls are set up in a city square. They sell fruit and vegetables, meat and fish. Musicians play to earn a few coins from the crowd.

This customer is a slave. She is choosing a goose to take home and cook for a special feast tonight.

A butcher chops up a pig's head in his shop. Only rich people can afford meat every day.

This woman is selling hot food for people to eat at home. Many houses do not have stoves for cooking.

AT THE BATHS

When Petronius has finished his work, he goes to the public bathhouse. There are lots of baths in Rome and they cost very little to use. Very few people have baths in their homes.

The baths are not just places for washing. They are good places to go to meet friends or do business. Some people go there to do exercises, walk in the gardens or read quietly.

PEOPLE LEAVE THEIR CLOTHES ON SHELVES IN THE CHANGING ROOM.

SOME PEOPLE LIVE IN THESE APARTMENTS.

COLD BATH FOR COOLING DOWN AND SWIMMING

CAKE SELLER

PEOPLE ENJOY WALKING IN THE GARDEN.

WRESTLERS

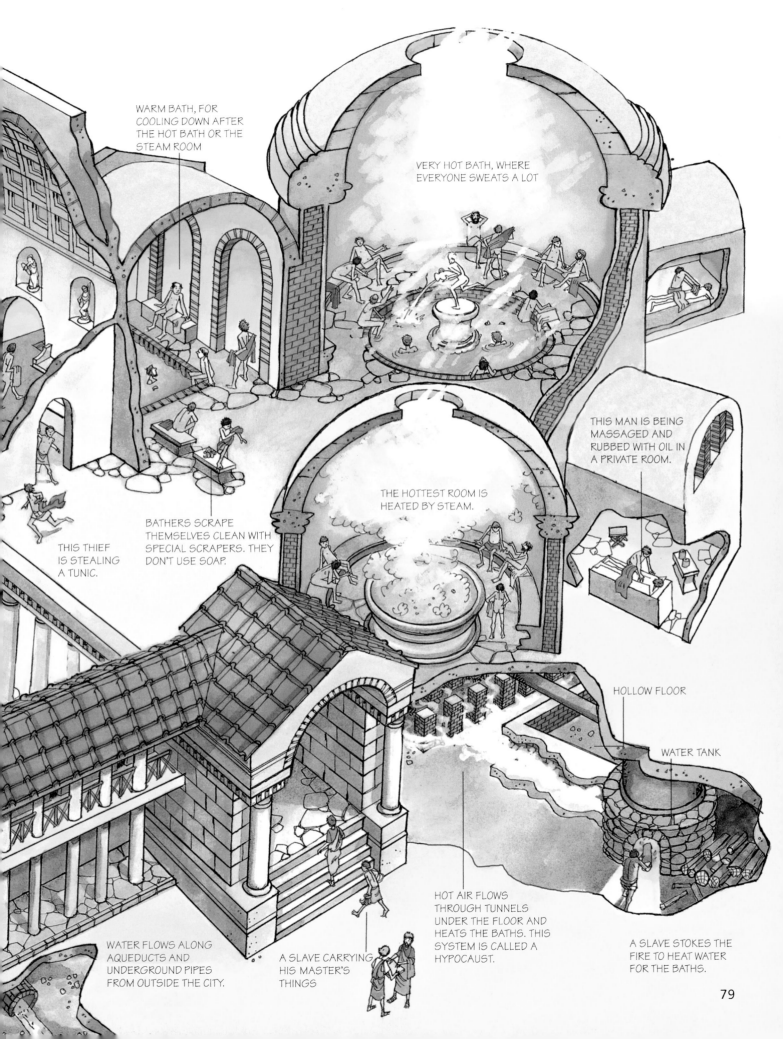

WARM BATH, FOR COOLING DOWN AFTER THE HOT BATH OR THE STEAM ROOM

VERY HOT BATH, WHERE EVERYONE SWEATS A LOT

THIS MAN IS BEING MASSAGED AND RUBBED WITH OIL IN A PRIVATE ROOM.

THE HOTTEST ROOM IS HEATED BY STEAM.

BATHERS SCRAPE THEMSELVES CLEAN WITH SPECIAL SCRAPERS. THEY DON'T USE SOAP.

THIS THIEF IS STEALING A TUNIC.

HOLLOW FLOOR

WATER TANK

WATER FLOWS ALONG AQUEDUCTS AND UNDERGROUND PIPES FROM OUTSIDE THE CITY.

A SLAVE CARRYING HIS MASTER'S THINGS

HOT AIR FLOWS THROUGH TUNNELS UNDER THE FLOOR AND HEATS THE BATHS. THIS SYSTEM IS CALLED A HYPOCAUST.

A SLAVE STOKES THE FIRE TO HEAT WATER FOR THE BATHS.

79

GAMES AND RACES

At festival time and on public holidays, Petronius takes his family to race tracks or arenas to be entertained.

In arenas, prisoners and criminals are put to death. Some are attacked by wild animals, others have to fight gladiators. Gladiators are men who have been sentenced to death. They train at special schools to fight and die bravely.

The biggest arena in the city of Rome is called the Colosseum. It is enormous and can seat up to 50,000 people.

WILD ANIMALS FROM ALL OVER THE EMPIRE ARE BROUGHT TO FIGHT.

THIS LION WAS CAPTURED IN NORTH AFRICA.

GLADIATOR CONTESTS

To make the fights more exciting, gladiators use a variety of weapons. This man has a net. He is dodging a sharp sword.

When he gets a chance, he flings his net over his opponent. He tries to tangle him up in it and stab him with a fisherman's spear.

The wounded man begs for mercy. If the crowd gives a "thumbs up" sign, he will live. A "thumbs down" means he must be killed.

THE CIRCUS

Chariot races are held at a huge track called the Circus. The horses race around the track seven times. Everyone shouts with excitement as the chariots speed past. The drivers are in four different teams – reds, greens, blues and whites

The winning driver is given a purse full of gold and treated like a hero.

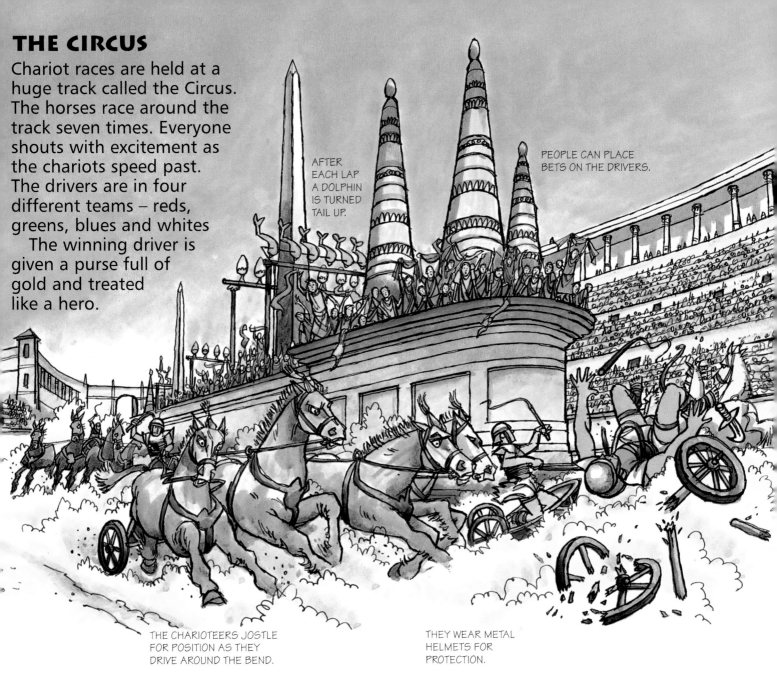

AFTER EACH LAP A DOLPHIN IS TURNED TAIL UP.

PEOPLE CAN PLACE BETS ON THE DRIVERS.

THE CHARIOTEERS JOSTLE FOR POSITION AS THEY DRIVE AROUND THE BEND.

THEY WEAR METAL HELMETS FOR PROTECTION.

A CHARIOT RACE

At the beginning of a race, the charioteers wait at the starting line. Each man leans forward to help balance the light chariot, which is made of wood and leather.

A trumpet sounds, the starter drops his white flag, and they are off. The reins are tied around the charioteers' waists, so they can lean back and whip their horses.

If a chariot crashes or a horse stumbles, the driver pulls out his dagger. He quickly cuts the reins to stop himself from being dragged along the ground by the horses.

BUILDING IN THE CITY

Rome is always filled with the sound of building. Old houses are pulled down, and new and bigger ones are put up in their places.

Today, some craftsmen are constructing a huge new aqueduct, while others are building a house for a wealthy Roman merchant.

THIS IS A NEW AQUEDUCT. IT WILL CARRY WATER TO BATHS AND FOUNTAINS IN THE CITY.

STONE BLOCKS

RUBBLE IS TAKEN AWAY.

THIS ARTIST IS PAINTING A PICTURE CALLED A MURAL ON WET PLASTER.

THIS MAN IS BUILDING A WALL OF BRICKS MADE OF BAKED CLAY.

ASSISTANT

THIS MAN IS PLASTERING A NEW WALL.

TILES

THESE MEN ARE MAKING A FLOOR OUT OF PIECES OF MARBLE.

CARVING A TOMBSTONE

This man is carving a tombstone. Even poor people save up to buy tombstones.

He is carving a portrait of the dead man, whose name was P. Licinius Philonicus.

The mason has carved pictures of tools on the stone to show that the man made coins.

THIS SCAFFOLDING WILL BE TAKEN AWAY WHEN THE ARCH IS COMPLETE.

A CRANE LIFTS HEAVY STONES UP TO THE TOPS OF THE COLUMNS.

STONE WORKERS, CALLED MASONS, CARVE PILLARS AND BIG STONES FOR TEMPLES AND PALACES.

WOODEN PLANKS FOR DOORS AND WINDOWS

CRANE

CARPENTERS

A MOSAIC FLOOR IS BEING LAID IN THIS ROOM.

WET PLASTER

HOW TO MAKE A MOSAIC

GLASS AND STONE

WET PLASTER

A craftsman spreads wet plaster over a small patch of the floor. Then he smooths it down.

He presses little squares of glass or stone into the plaster. Little by little, he makes up a picture.

When the picture is finished, he rubs more plaster all over it to fill in the small gaps between the squares.

PETRONIUS GIVES A FEAST

Tonight, Petronius has asked some friends to dinner. All day, his servants and slaves have been hard at work in the kitchen preparing delicious food.

The guests are lying on couches and eating the food with their fingers. Petronius's servants make sure that they all have plenty of wine to drink.

Servants can't afford to eat fish or meat. Instead, they have dull food, such as porridge made from wheat. Sometimes, Petronius holds a special feast for them.

SLAVES CARRY A LADY TO THE FEAST IN A BOX CALLED A LITTER.

THIS GUEST IS LATE. THE ROMANS ONLY HAVE SUN DIALS AND HOUR GLASSES, SO IT'S HARD TO BE ON TIME.

ROASTING MEAT OVER A FIRE

VEGETABLES AND SAUCES ARE COOKED ON A STOVE.

THE KITCHEN IS HOT, DARK, DIRTY AND VERY BUSY.

TWO SLAVES PLAY DICE WHILE WAITING FOR THEIR MASTER, WHO IS ONE OF THE GUESTS.

COOKING

FISH HERBS WINE HONEY PEPPER

The head cook is making sauce for a meat dish. He pounds up the insides of fish with some herbs, spices, wine and honey.

BEANS PEAS MARROWS ONIONS LETTUCE

Two slaves chop up beans, onions, asparagus, lettuce and garlic. The vegetables will be eaten raw for the first course.

SNAILS OYSTERS

Live snails left in milk for two days have grown fat. One slave takes them out of their shells, while another slave opens oysters.

IN THE DINING ROOM

LESS IMPORTANT GUESTS EAT CHEAPER FOOD AT THIS TABLE.

OIL LAMP

THIS IS THE CHIEF GUEST. HE IS BUSY DICTATING LETTERS TO HIS SECRETARY WHILE HE EATS.

A PIPE

THIS MAN IS TELLING A STORY ABOUT HIS RECENT TRIP TO BRITAIN.

THIS SLAVE IS POURING PETRONIUS SOME WINE.

THIS MAN IS PLAYING A CITHERA.

A POET WAITS TO RECITE POEMS.

THE MOST IMPORTANT GUESTS SIT AT THE MAIN TABLE AND HAVE THE NICEST FOOD.

GUESTS WASH THEIR HANDS BETWEEN COURSES.

FIRST COURSE

OIL AND EGG SAUCE

STUFFED DORMICE

PEACOCKS' EGGS

The first course is a dish of stuffed and cooked dormice, stuffed olives and prunes, and peacocks' eggs with a sauce.

MAIN COURSE

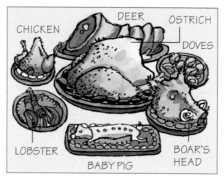

CHICKEN

DEER

OSTRICH

DOVES

LOBSTER

BABY PIG

BOAR'S HEAD

Boiled and roasted meat is served for the second course. It is sliced by the slaves, as the guests don't have any knives or forks.

THIRD COURSE

FRUIT

HONEY CAKES

STUFFED DATES

The last course is fruit, dates and cakes sweetened with honey. After this, the guests drink a toast to each other's health.

SUMMER ON THE FARM

During the summer, Rome is a very hot and smelly place. So Petronius has decided to take his family and servants to the countryside for a few weeks. He owns a big house, called a villa, which stands in the middle of his farmland.

September is a very busy time on the farm. Grapes and olives have to be picked and made into wine and oil. All kinds of food have to be collected and stored, so they can be eaten during the winter.

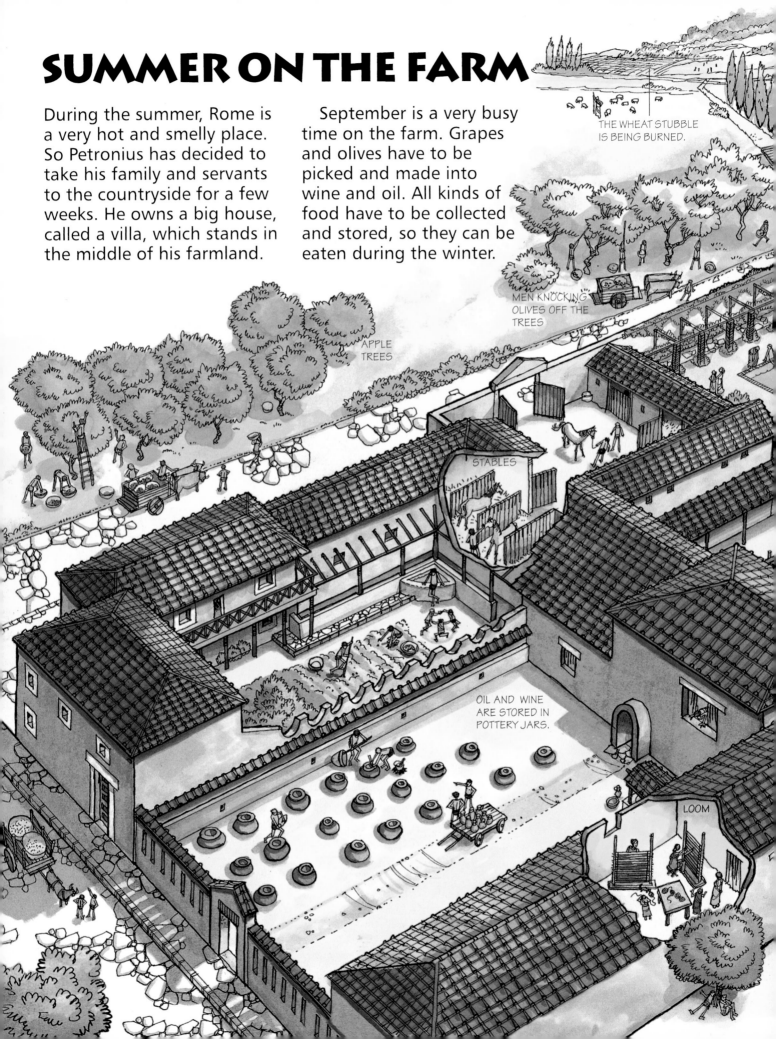

THE WHEAT STUBBLE IS BEING BURNED.

MEN KNOCKING OLIVES OFF THE TREES

APPLE TREES

STABLES

OIL AND WINE ARE STORED IN POTTERY JARS.

LOOM

PAYING THE RENT

Local peasants farm Petronius's land for him. They pay rent for the land with money, or with the food they have grown, or with animals. The farm manager writes down what they pay.

PRESSING OLIVES

When the olives have been harvested, they are put into a screw press. Workers wind the handles to squash the olives and squeeze out the oil.

WILLOW TREES

GOATS' MILK WILL BE MADE INTO TASTY CHEESE.

PETRONIUS

PIGS

BUNCHES OF RIPE GRAPES

HENS

GEESE

WELL

MANURE

BEEHIVES MADE OF THIN, WOVEN TWIGS

GRAPEVINES

FIG TREE

A SLAVE IS WEAVING BASKETS OUT OF STICKS CUT FROM THE WILLOW TREES BY THE RIVER.

MAKING WINE

Grapes are poured into a stone trough. Men tread on them to squash out the juice. They hold sticks to stop them from slipping over on the mushy grape skins.

The grape skins are then put into a press to squeeze out the rest of the juice. The juice is put into big jars. It bubbles and foams as it turns into wine.

MARCUS JOINS THE ARMY

Petronius's son Marcus has joined the Roman army, and has been sent to a camp with other new recruits. While he is at the camp, Marcus will be taught all the things soldiers have to know when fighting Rome's enemies.

Marcus and the other new soldiers have their names written down in the army record book. They have to swear an oath and promise to be loyal to the emperor. They will swear this oath again every year.

LIFE IN THE CAMP

Marcus is measured by an army tailor who will make his uniform. Marcus has to wear a tunic, and a breast plate made of metal and leather.

Next, he tries on several bronze helmets to find one which is the right size. The helmets are lined with leather to protect soldiers' heads.

The training will make the new recruits strong and good at fighting. They start with marching twice a day, carrying spears and heavy packs.

Marcus learns to fight by running at a target with a wooden sword. Sometimes, he and the other boys fight each other with swords and spears in mock battles.

Horse riding is fun, but everyone laughs when Marcus falls off. There are no stirrups for his feet, so it is hard to balance in the saddle while carrying a heavy shield.

The recruits learn to lock their shields together to make a formation called a "tortoise". This will protect them from enemy arrows and stones, but it is not easy for beginners.

SOLDIERS AT WORK

The recruits learn how to make a camp out of turf and wooden stakes. This will be useful when they are marching through enemy territory.

CLAY FOR TILES

OVEN

BAKED TILES

STONE CUTTING

They learn how to use mallets and chisels to cut and shape stones. They are also taught how to bake clay roof tiles in an oven.

To build roads, they dig wide ditches and fill them with stones. Flat stones go on top. The roads slope down on each side so water runs off them.

THE ARMY CAMP

The army camp is huge, and it is surrounded by strong stone walls. Outside the walls, a little town has been built. There are houses and market stalls, and people farm the land.

They sell the food they grow and the clothes they make to the troops.

Sometimes the soldiers' families come to live outside the camp.

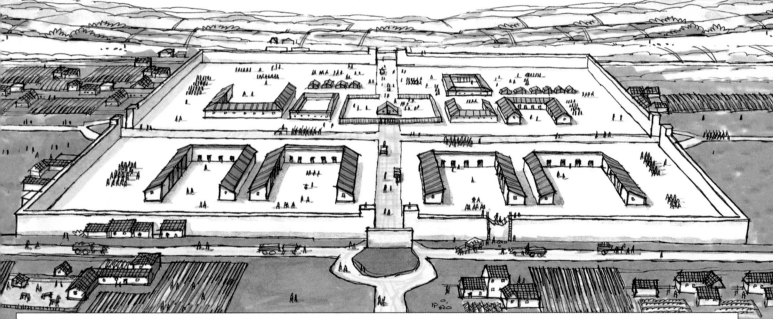

FIRING A CATAPULT

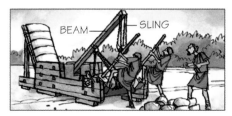

BEAM — SLING

Today, Marcus is being taught how to fire a catapult. He and his friend, Maximus, wind down the catapult's huge beam, which has a sling at one end.

Then, a man known as a loader lifts a large, round stone and fits it into the sling. This stone can weigh as much as 30 kilos (about 66 pounds).

When the soldiers fire the catapult, the stone is flung high into the air and lands up to 30m (100ft) away. It can easily smash holes in the walls of enemy forts.

ATTACK!

Marcus has finished his training and is now a junior officer. He has marched with a large army to Romania, in Eastern Europe. The Dacians, who live here, have been threatening Roman lands.

Some Dacian soldiers have retreated to a hilltop fort, called a citadel. The Romans, who have set up camp nearby, are attacking the citadel.

THE SOLDIERS HAVE BUILT A BRIDGE FROM PLANKS ON TOP OF BOATS.

THE ROMANS HAVE BUILT A JETTY FOR UNLOADING SUPPLIES.

MULES CARRYING SUPPLIES TO THE ROMAN CAMP.

A SEARCH PARTY RETURNS FROM SEARCHING THE FOREST FOR ENEMY FIGHTERS.

A STANDARD BEARER LEADS THE WAY.

MEN REAPING DACIAN CORN FOR FOOD TO FEED THE ROMAN ARMY

SHIELDS

THE ROMAN CAMP

THIS MAN IS MAKING A LIST OF THE NEW SUPPLIES.

STANDARD

FOOD SUPPLIES

TEN MEN SLEEP IN EACH OF THESE LEATHER TENTS.

COOKS ARE ROASTING AN OX THAT WAS CAPTURED FROM THE DACIAN HERD.

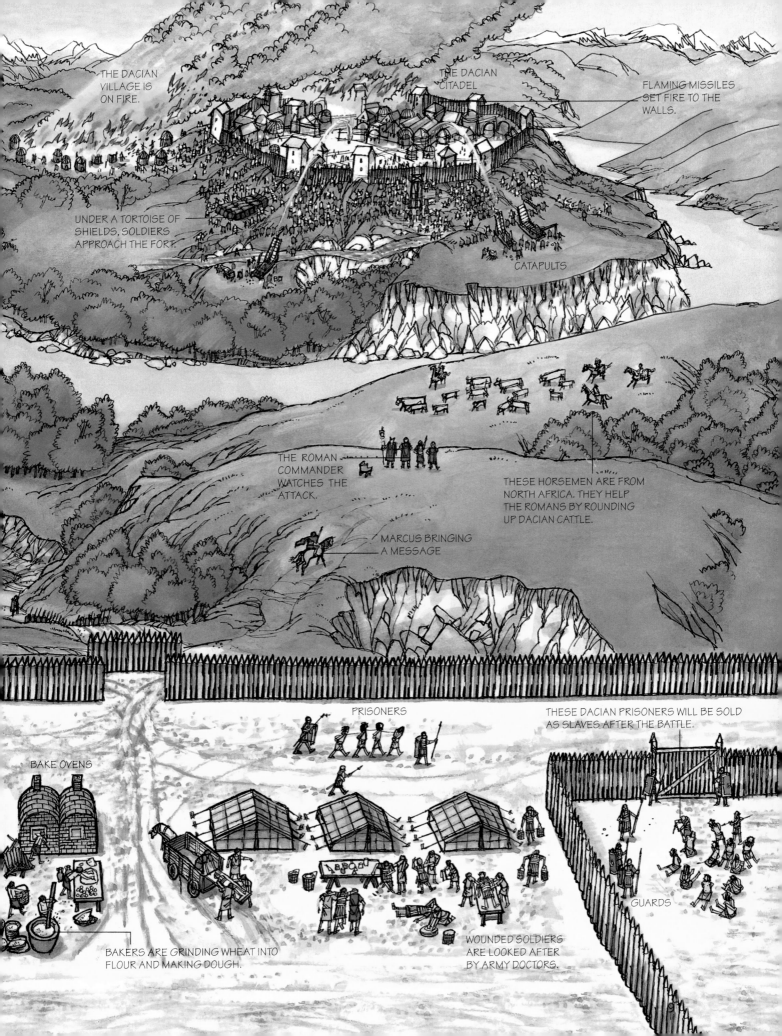

THE DACIAN VILLAGE IS ON FIRE.

THE DACIAN CITADEL

FLAMING MISSILES SET FIRE TO THE WALLS.

UNDER A TORTOISE OF SHIELDS, SOLDIERS APPROACH THE FORT.

CATAPULTS

THE ROMAN COMMANDER WATCHES THE ATTACK.

THESE HORSEMEN ARE FROM NORTH AFRICA. THEY HELP THE ROMANS BY ROUNDING UP DACIAN CATTLE.

MARCUS BRINGING A MESSAGE

PRISONERS

THESE DACIAN PRISONERS WILL BE SOLD AS SLAVES AFTER THE BATTLE.

BAKE OVENS

GUARDS

BAKERS ARE GRINDING WHEAT INTO FLOUR AND MAKING DOUGH.

WOUNDED SOLDIERS ARE LOOKED AFTER BY ARMY DOCTORS.

THE ROMAN EMPIRE

This map shows how the Roman empire looked a few years after your trip to Ancient Rome. It covered most of Europe and surrounded the Mediterranean Sea. All the areas shown in green on this map were part of the empire.

The map also shows what food and goods were brought to Rome and how they got there.

THE ROMANS BELIEVED THERE WERE TERRIBLE MONSTERS IN THE SEA.

BRITAIN

London

R. Elbe

Cologne

R. Rhine

ATLANTIC OCEAN

FRANCE

ALPS

Pyrenees

Ravenna

SPAIN

Marseilles

Rome
Ostia

ITALY

SARDINIA

Cartegna

Carthage

Leptis Magna

LIBYA

ALL THE THINGS BROUGHT TO ROME

FRUIT		SHEEP		JEWELS		GLASS		CLOTH	
WINE		HORSES		GOLD		POTTERY		PURPLE DYE	
HONEY		WILD ANIMALS		AMBER		LAMPS		PARCHMENT	
GRAIN		HIDES		SILVER		TIN		MARBLE	
OLIVES		TIMBER		BRONZE FURNITURE		LEAD		SLAVES	

THE BARBARIANS INVADE

The Romans called the people who lived outside their empire "barbarians", meaning foreigners. Some barbarians were wandering tribes. They moved about, looking for new land to farm and graze their animals. Sometimes they attacked Roman frontiers to reach the land inside the empire.

In the 4th century AD, thousands of barbarians invaded Roman lands from the northeast. They burned towns and cities, destroyed farms and killed people.

The empire gradually grew smaller. The Roman armies were driven back. The emperors couldn't get enough men or money to fight the invaders. In AD410, the barbarians captured Rome itself.

Barbarians

Barbarians

R. Drieper

Slaves

CASPIAN SEA

ROMANIA (DACIA)

R. Danube

BLACK SEA

Salt

GREECE

Constantinople

Shipbuilding

Camel train

SYRIA

Silk from China

Athens

Dura-Europos

Antioch

Palmyra

CYPRUS

Sidon

Damascus

CRETE

Tyre

MEDITERRANEAN SEA

JUDEA

Grain ships

Petra

Alexandria

Cano

EGYPT

R. Nile

RED SEA

WHAT'S LEFT TODAY?

All over Europe and North Africa are the remains of Roman towns, villas, forts and baths; so you can see exactly where the Romans lived nearly 2,000 years ago. The long straight roads they built were so well made that some are still used today.

THE STORY OF ROME

In about 753BC (753 years before Jesus was born), a tribe from Northern Europe built a village on a hill near the Tiber River in Italy. They began to farm, and gradually the village grew into a city. Rome was ruled by kings.

SETTLING BY THE TIBER

In 509BC, the people decided they didn't want to be ruled by a king any more. Instead, every year they chose two men, called consuls, to rule. The Romans fought to protect their land, and captured more and more territory. By 250BC, they ruled the whole of Italy.

CONQUERING AN EMPIRE

In 206BC, war broke out with a sea-going people from Carthage, North Africa. The Romans built a huge fleet of ships and won great battles. The Carthaginians made a new base in Spain.

FIGHTING THE CARTHAGINIANS

A Carthaginian soldier named Hannibal gathered a huge army. Many of Rome's enemies joined him. They used elephants to cross over the Alps from Spain into Italy. Hannibal won many battles. But the Romans cut off his food supplies, so he couldn't reach Rome.

HANNIBAL'S ARMY

In 204BC, the Romans attacked Carthage. Hannibal sailed home to defend it, but he was defeated. Later, the Romans besieged the city and completely destroyed it. The people were killed or sold as slaves.

ATTACKING CARTHAGE

The Romans became the most powerful people in the Mediterranean. In Rome, the rich lived in great luxury. But many government officials became greedy and corrupt. The rulers of some areas of the empire demanded huge taxes from their subjects.

LIVING IN LUXURY

Civil war broke out in Rome when two generals tried to grab power. One marched his troops through the streets, killing everyone he didn't like. In 73BC, a slave named Spartacus led a revolt. He escaped to Mount Vesuvius, joined by 90,000 slaves. He fought off the Roman army until he was killed in 71BC.

SPARTACUS AND HIS SLAVE ARMY

Two generals, Caesar and Pompey, struggled to control the government. Caesar marched from Gaul to Rome, but Pompey left for Greece. Caesar defeated Pompey's army and Pompey escaped to Egypt, where he was murdered. Caesar went to Egypt and helped Queen Cleopatra hold on to her throne. After more conquests, he returned to Rome.

In 45BC, Caesar became sole ruler of Rome. He encouraged justice and planned to improve the city. But his enemies feared he would try to become king, so they murdered him in 44BC.

CAESAR'S MURDER

Caesar's heir, Octavian, defeated his rival Mark Antony in a sea battle. Antony and his wife, Cleopatra, killed themselves rather than face their defeat.

CLEOPATRA DYING

Octavian, Rome's first emperor, took the name Augustus. He strengthened the army and extended the empire. But he was defeated by German tribes. Throughout the empire, people built cities and roads. It was a time of peace and successful trade.

Augustus was succeeded by members of his family. But an emperor wasn't like a king. Anyone who had enough support could come to power. For example, in one year there were four different emperors. Later, men who weren't even born in Rome became emperors.

In AD117, a great general named Hadrian became emperor. He strengthened the frontiers and built a stone wall across northern Britain to keep out barbarian tribes. In Judea, the Roman army put down a revolt by the Jews and thousands were killed.

HADRIAN'S WALL

In the 2nd century AD the Roman empire reached its greatest extent. But the barbarians were attacking its frontiers. Southern German tribes attacked northern Italy. They were defeated, but still threatened the northern and eastern borders of the empire.

BARBARIANS ATTACK

In the 3rd century, the army dominated the government and chose emperors. The empire was too vast to control, and there were many civil wars. Old enemies, such as the Persians, began to regain land they had lost. Emperor Valerian was defeated and killed.

VALERIAN SUBMITS

People feared that Rome couldn't protect them from the barbarians. Soldiers posted across the empire spread new religions, such as Christianity. Emperors blamed the Christians for troubles in the empire, and put many Christians to death.

CHRISTIANS KILLED

In AD284, Diocletian, an army general, was declared emperor by his troops. He made the empire easier to control by dividing it into two halves, an eastern and western half. But there still wasn't enough money to pay the armies needed to fight off barbarian invaders.

Emperor Constantine made Christianity the state religion in AD320. He set up a new capital called Constantinople, from where he ruled the eastern half of the empire.

The barbarians invaded the western empire and destroyed Rome in AD410. They rapidly invaded the rest of Italy.

ROME IS RANSACKED

A barbarian became ruler of Italy in AD476. Constantinople held off its enemies until it was captured by Turks in AD1453.

Although the Roman empire was destroyed, the Romans have influenced many things in the modern world, including Western law and architecture. The languages now spoken in France, Spain, Portugal and Italy all developed from Latin – the Roman language. There are also many Latin words in Dutch, German and English.

ROME & ROMANS
TIME QUIZ

1. What is the name of the river on which the city of Rome is built?
2. What is a forum?
3. What is the name of the robe that men who are citizens of Rome are allowed to wear?
4. What is the underground system of tunnels used to heat a bathhouse called?
5. What are the prisoners who are trained to fight each other to entertain the crowds called?
6. What is the name of the biggest arena in Rome which holds up to 50,000 people?
7. How many times do the charioteers drive around the track at the Circus?
8. What does an aqueduct carry?
9. What do Petronius's guests use to eat their food at the feast?
10. What is a tortoise formation?

Answers on page 130.

NEXT STOP
PHARAOHS & PYRAMIDS

Contents

BACK TO ANCIENT EGYPT

Your final journey through time will take you to Ancient Egypt. The Ancient Egyptians were among the first people to leave behind pictures and writings showing how they lived. It is by looking at these things that we know what Ancient Egypt was like.

To travel in time from Ancient Rome to Ancient Egypt, you need to go back another one and a half thousand years. This is your longest journey yet. It will take you to a time 1,400 years before Jesus was born.

Dates of events that happened before Jesus are written like this: 1400 BC.

When you have finished your visit, and you want to come back to the present again, just press the Emergency Getaway Button on your helmet.

1. SET YOUR TIME HELMET

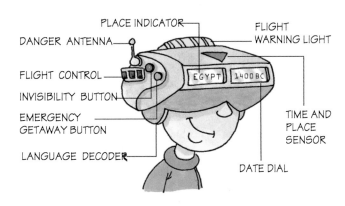

For your final journey you need to change the time and destination on your time travel helmet. Set the Date Dial to the year "1400 BC". Make sure your remember to make it BC. Next, set the Place Indicator to "Egypt".

2. YOUR DESTINATION

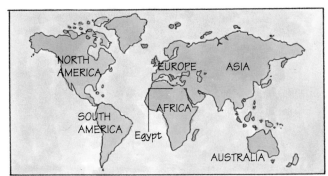

Egypt is in the top right-hand corner of the continent we now call Africa.

Below you can see the house of Petronius that you are leaving and the palace of the Egyptian Pharaoh you will meet on your new visit.

3. GO!

One moment you are with Petronius and his wife Livia, the next, you are off, whizzing through space, going back one and a half thousand years in time. Make sure you adjust your Language Decoder so you can understand what the people of Ancient Egypt are saying.

In just a few seconds you arrive at the court of the Pharaoh of Egypt. He is sitting with his wife in his splendid palace. They are playing a board game called *senit*. They are both dressed in their crowns and robes.

THE PEOPLE YOU WILL MEET

All Egyptians live within a few miles of a river called the Nile. The weather is warm and sunny most of the time, so they don't need to wear many clothes. Children hardly ever wear anything at all.

Rich people have pleasant lives. They have servants and slaves to do much of the work. But most of the people in Egypt are poor peasants who have to work hard to live.

The Vizier is Pharaoh's chief helper. It is his job to see that Pharaoh's orders are carried out.

Most Egyptians are peasants. They have to grow enough food to live on, and pay taxes to Pharaoh's officials. If they fail to pay they are beaten.

Priests work in the temples, looking after the gods. To keep themselves pure and clean, they bathe four times a day, shave their bodies, and dress in the finest white linen.

Pharaoh is the ruler of all Egypt. His subjects believe that he is a god in the body of a man. They think that he can do no wrong.

Soldiers lead hard, dangerous lives. But a few successful ones may become rich and famous generals.

Most servants are free to leave their masters if they want, but others are slaves. Slaves are usually foreigners who were captured in wars.

NAKHT AND HIS FAMILY

The main people you will meet in this book are Nakht and his family. They live in a big house on the Nile near a city named Memphis.

NAKHT

TIY

Nakht and Tiy have been married for 20 years. Nakht is a wealthy landowner and he is in charge of a local temple's land. Tiy is in charge of looking after the house and taking care of the children.

MOSI

SHERY

HORI

MEU

AHMOSE

Mosi, the eldest son, is 16. Nakht wanted him to work in the temple, but Mosi wants to be a soldier. Nakht has finally agreed to this, and has promised to introduce him to a general he knows.

Shery, the eldest daughter, is 13. Because she is a girl, she doesn't go to school. Instead she is taught what she needs to know at home. This includes singing and dancing.

Hori, the youngest son, is 10. He goes to a school in a temple in Memphis, where he learns to read and write. He expects to take over his father's job after Nakht has retired.

The youngest daughter is called Meu, which means "kitten". She is 8 years old. After her lessons, she spends most of the day playing outside in the sunshine.

Ahmose, Nakht's nephew, is staying with his uncle's family. His own father has gone on a long trading voyage to Byblos, a port across the Mediterranean Sea in Lebanon.

A TRIP TO ANCIENT EGYPT

The date is 1400 BC. You are hovering above Egypt. Beneath you are miles of desert through which runs a very long and wide river, called the Nile.

MEDITERRANEAN SEA

RED SEA

WOOD FROM BYBLOS UP THE COAST

WANDERING SHEPHERDS COME THIS WAY TO FEED THEIR FLOCKS.

CARAVANS BRING COPPER AND TURQUOISE – A LOVELY BLUE SEMI-PRECIOUS STONE.

TRIBESMEN CALLED BEDOUIN LIVE HERE.

COPPER AND TURQUOISE ARE MINED HERE.

GOLD, GRAIN AND PAPYRUS FROM EGYPT

BORDER FORTS

HELIOPOLIS

THE GREAT BITTER LAKE

STONE FOR THE PYRAMIDS WAS QUARRIED HERE.

THE RED LAND

PEOPLE ONLY GO TO THE DESERT TO HUNT, TRADE OR MINE.

EGYPTIANS TRAVEL ALONG THE NILE BY BOAT.

ALABASTER USED FOR

BUBASTIS

THE DELTA

SAIS

MEMPHIS (OLD CAPITAL OF EGYPT)

LAKE MAREOTIS

THE FAYUM

THE RED LAND

SAND DWELLERS WANDER THROUGH THE DESERT.

POLICE PATROL THE WESTERN DESERT WITH HOUNDS.

The Great Pyramid and the Sphinx

The Step Pyramid

Nobles hunt gazelles here

The Temple of Karnak

COPTOS

THEBES (CAPITAL OF EGYPT)

GOLD IS MINED IN THESE HILLS.

DENDERA

ABYDOS

Deir el Bahari

The Valley of the Kings

1ST CATARACT

ASWAN – GRANITE FOR BUILDINGS AND STATUES IS QUARRIED HERE.

THIS AREA IS CALLED WAWAT.

GOLD FROM WAWAT.

GOLD IS MINED HERE.

THE RED LAND

SOUTH OF THE CATARACT LIE THE LANDS OF NUBIA AND KUSH.

DIORITE – A STONE USED FOR STATUES IS QUARRIED HERE.

BUHEN

2ND CATARACT

THE NUBIANS OF KUSH WERE CONQUERED YEARS AGO BUT SOME STILL REBEL FROM TIME TO TIME.

Without the Nile, no one could live in Egypt because there is very little rain. Every year the river floods its banks. When the waters go down, they leave a strip of land on which crops grow well.

The Egyptians call the river valley the Black Land, because of its black soil. Here they build villages, towns and temples. The capital city is called Thebes.

In an area called the Delta, the river splits into many channels to reach the sea. Lots of people live here because there is plenty of water.

The desert all around is called the Red Land. Only wild animals and a few people live there. The Egyptians bury their dead in the desert on the west bank of the Nile. There are great monuments and tombs, including the pyramids and the Valleys of the Kings and Queens.

The Egyptians call the sea the Great Green. Trading ships sail down the Red Sea to the mysterious land of Punt, on the African coast.

ALONG THE NILE

It is late in the year and the farmers are busy sowing seeds for next year's harvest.

Another urgent job is to repair the canal banks. Canals are used for travel and to carry water to fields far from the Nile.

There is very little rain, so water can't be wasted. Large pools called catch-basins are built to store flood water, so it can be used throughout the year to water the fields.

The Nile itself is busy with traffic. It is Egypt's main highway. Statues and stones for building are carried down the river in ships and barges.

Nakht's boat has just turned off the river. He is going home to his house.

STATUE OF PTAH FOR A TEMPLE

FISHERMEN IN BOATS MADE OF PAPYRUS REEDS

NAKHT'S BOAT IS MADE OF WOOD.

NAKHT

ROPE STRETCHERS REMEASURING THE FIELDS.

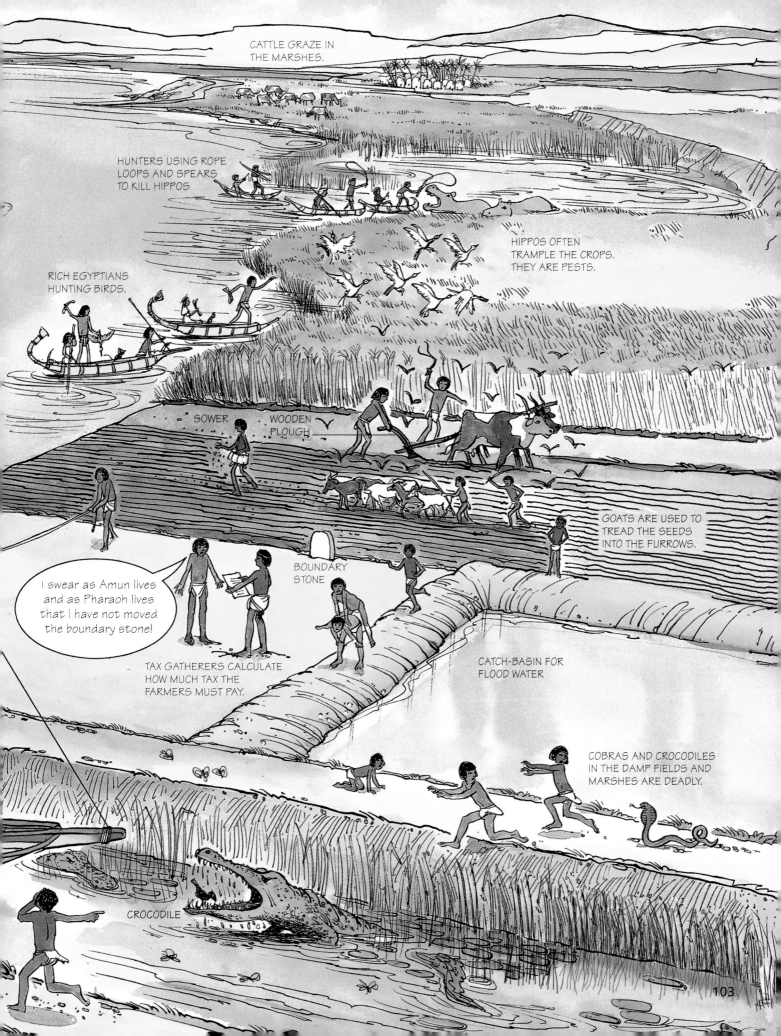

AT HOME WITH NAKHT

Nakht lives with his family near the Nile. He owns a house, a stableyard and some small buildings where his servants live and where food is cooked.

Nakht has a lot of land around his house. Peasants farm this land, and in return they give Nakht some of the food they grow. A steward makes sure that the peasants give Nakht all that they owe him.

Nakht's house is built with bricks made of mud mixed with straw. Inside, the house is cool and shady, but the family spend a lot of time outdoors in the sunshine.

Nakht's slaves and gardeners look after the grounds around the house.

COLLECTING HONEY FROM BEEHIVES

NAKHT

TIY

PILLARED ROOM FOR RECEIVING NAKHT'S IMPORTANT GUESTS

WORKMEN PICK FIGS WITH THE HELP OF PET BABOONS.

THIS MAN DIDN'T BRING ENOUGH GEESE.

DUCKS' EGGS

NAKHT'S STEWARD

PEASANTS BRING CATTLE AND GEESE TO THE STEWARD.

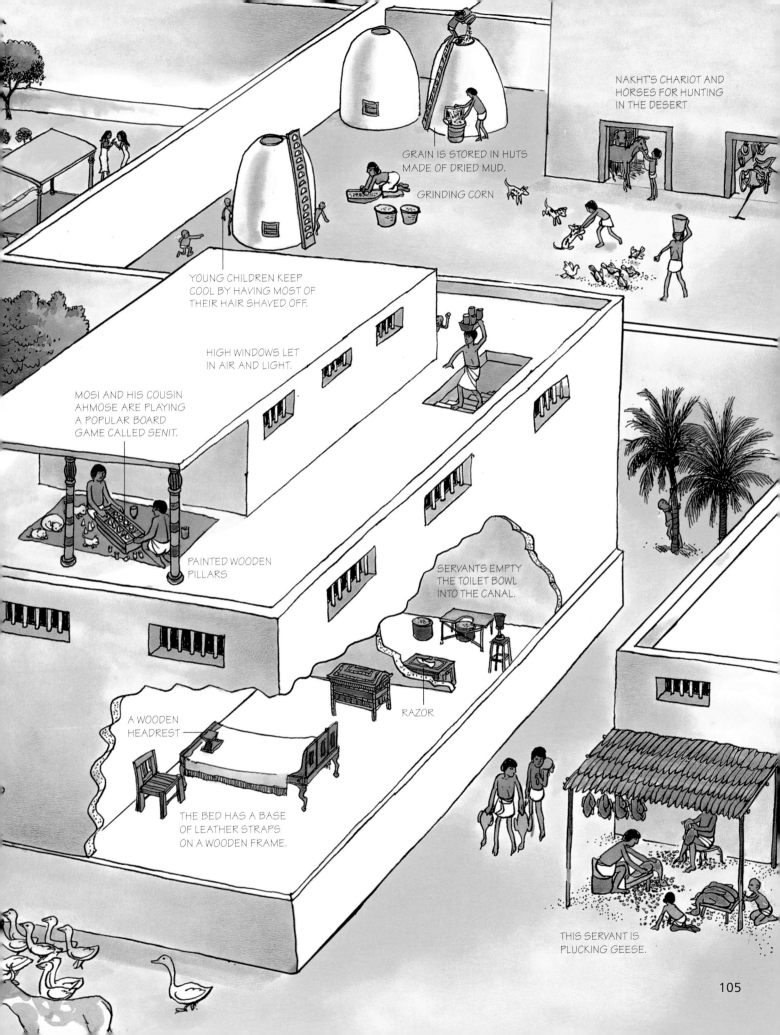

NAKHT'S CHARIOT AND HORSES FOR HUNTING IN THE DESERT

GRAIN IS STORED IN HUTS MADE OF DRIED MUD.

GRINDING CORN

YOUNG CHILDREN KEEP COOL BY HAVING MOST OF THEIR HAIR SHAVED OFF.

HIGH WINDOWS LET IN AIR AND LIGHT.

MOSI AND HIS COUSIN AHMOSE ARE PLAYING A POPULAR BOARD GAME CALLED SENIT.

PAINTED WOODEN PILLARS

SERVANTS EMPTY THE TOILET BOWL INTO THE CANAL.

RAZOR

A WOODEN HEADREST

THE BED HAS A BASE OF LEATHER STRAPS ON A WOODEN FRAME.

THIS SERVANT IS PLUCKING GEESE.

105

A FEAST

Nakht is giving a feast to celebrate his return home. The Egyptians love parties.

The guests are gathered in the central hall of Nakht's house. Married couples sit together, but unmarried boys and girls have to sit apart.

Servants bring food and wine to the guests, while dancers and musicians entertain them. After the dancing, a harpist sings one of Egypt's oldest songs. The words tell people to make the most of their lives, because life is only a dream, and everyone will die one day.

THE GUESTS EAT THE FOOD WITH THEIR FINGERS AND THEN WASH THEM IN BOWLS OF WATER.

SOME GUESTS WEAR LOTUS BLOSSOMS IN THEIR HAIR.

SERVANTS OFFER FOOD AND POUR WINE.

PET GOOSE

PREPARING FOOD

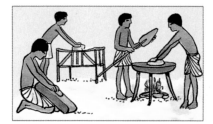

Nakht's servants are busy baking bread and a variety of cakes for the guests at the feast to enjoy.

Ducks and geese make popular meat courses. They are roasted over an open fire. The cook fans the flames to keep them burning.

FIGS

HONEYCOMB

DATES

Vegetables and fruit, including figs, dates and grapes, are grown on Nakht's land. Honey is used to sweeten drinks and food.

SHERY GETS READY FOR THE FEAST

Holding her bronze mirror, Shery rims her eyes with a black powder called kohl.

She grinds red clay into a powder to rub on her cheeks and palms.

A servant helps Shery put on her wig. On top of it she places a cone of perfumed oil.

PERFUME CONES MELT, DRENCHING PEOPLE'S HAIR WITH SWEET-SMELLING OILS.

HARPIST

DANCERS

WINE JAR

PET MONKEY

MAKING WINE

Most Egyptians drink beer, but rich people are also fond of wine. Landowners often grow grapes on trellises like these.

The grapes are taken to the press. While some workers trample them underfoot, others collect the juice that gushes out.

The juice is poured into pottery jars to ferment into wine. These are sealed with a cap of mud and leaves which dry in the sun.

VISITING A TEMPLE

The temple in which Nakht works is like a small city. It has workshops, a school, a library, storerooms and granaries. Outside its walls, there are acres of farmland that belong to the temple.

The Egyptians believe that temples are the homes of gods. The most important part of a temple is a small room that only priests enter.

It is the sanctuary where the god lives.

Ordinary people are not allowed into the sanctuary. They can go to the temple to make offerings to the god or to work.

Today, Hori has come to learn how to read and write at the temple school.

A votive tablet. People buy them to offer to the gods, hoping the gods will listen to their prayers.

CHIEF PRIEST'S HOUSE

SACRED LAKE, WHERE PRIESTS BATHE BEFORE CEREMONIES

FLAGPOLE

THE HYPOSTYLE HALL HAS BIG PILLARS.

STATUE OF PHARAOH

HORI

AN OBELISK. ITS TOP IS COVERED WITH GOLD.

MAKING AN OFFERING

THESE TOWERS FORM A GATEWAY CALLED A PYLON.

SETTING UP BOOTHS FOR A TEMPLE FESTIVAL

SONS OF TEMPLE OFFICIALS LEARN TO READ AND WRITE.

THE GODS OF EGYPT

The Egyptians believe in many different gods. All Egyptians worship the great gods, like Amun. But each city has a god of its own, who lives in the local temple.

Here are three gods that all Egyptians worship.

Amun of Thebes was the king of the gods

Ptah, the god of Memphis, and the god of craftsmen

Bes, a dwarf god, brings luck and happiness at home.

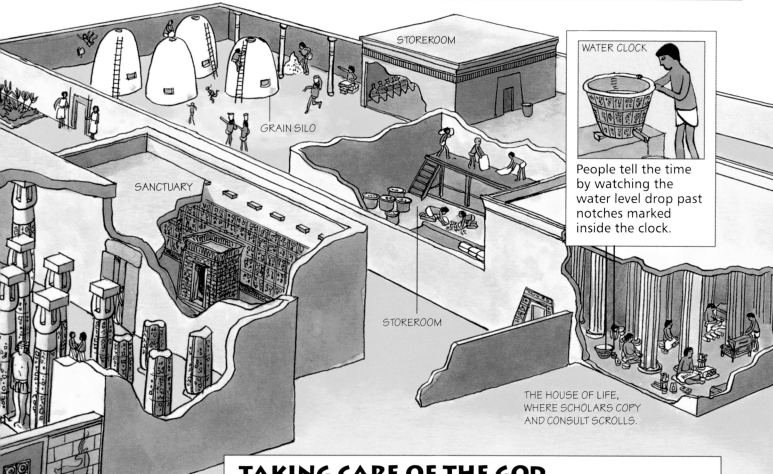

STOREROOM

GRAIN SILO

SANCTUARY

STOREROOM

WATER CLOCK

People tell the time by watching the water level drop past notches marked inside the clock.

THE HOUSE OF LIFE, WHERE SCHOLARS COPY AND CONSULT SCROLLS.

MUSICIANS PLAYING THEIR INSTRUMENTS

SCHOOLROOM

TAKING CARE OF THE GOD

Each morning a priest, who has just shaved and washed, enters the sanctuary. It is his job to look after the god.

He takes the god's statue out of its shrine. He sprinkles water on it, changes its clothing and then offers it food and drink.

Finally, he puts it back in the shrine and leaves the doors open until evening. As he goes out, he wipes away his footprints.

GOING TO SCHOOL

Most Egyptian children never go to school. As soon as they are old enough, the boys go to work with their fathers and the girls are taught how to run a home.

Hori goes to school because he wants to be a scribe at the temple, like his father Nakht. A scribe is someone who is specially trained to read and write.

Today, Hori and his schoolfriends are writing on pieces of stone or broken pottery called *ostraca*. The brushes they use to sketch writing symbols are made from reeds.

Hori doesn't like school much. There are no sports or games, and the teacher is very strict. Sometimes he beats lazy pupils with his cane. But Nakht tells Hori that if he studies, he will become wise, rich and successful.

A CASE CONTAINING SCROLLS OF A KIND OF PAPER CALLED PAPYRUS

HORI HARD AT WORK

CANE

WATER JUG

INKSTAND

REED BRUSH

RAG FOR ERASING MISTAKES

OSTRACA

MAKING PAPYRUS

The Egyptians use papyrus reeds to make paper. The reeds grow in marshy ground. Workers cut them down and carry them away to a workshop.

First, the long reeds are chopped into short lengths. Then the green outer skin is peeled away. The white pith inside is cut lengthways into wafer-thin slices.

MALLET FOR BEATING

CLOTH

POLISHING STONE

Two layers of pith are placed crossways on a block. A man places a cloth over them, and beats them into flat sheets. The sheets are polished smooth with a stone.

EGYPTIAN WRITING

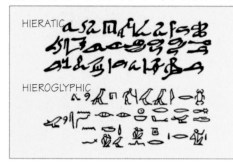

HIERATIC

HIEROGLYPHIC

WORD SIGNS

OLD MAN   JACKAL

SUN   HILL/FOREIGN LANDS

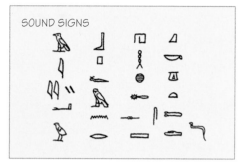

SOUND SIGNS

The Egyptians have two kinds of writing – hieratic and hieroglyphic. Hieratic is a kind of shorthand, used for day-to-day business. Hieroglyphic writing is used for religious writings and inscriptions on monuments. It is very difficult to learn.

Hori will be a temple scribe, so he has to learn hieroglyphic writing. Hieroglyphic writing is already about 2,000 years old. At first it was a picture language with a drawing for each word. A little drawing of a boat meant "boat".

Later, signs were used to stand for sounds, as the letters in our alphabet do. Words could be made up of several different signs. The picture above shows the main sound signs, but other signs are also used for groups of letters.

LEARNING TO READ HIEROGLYPHS

Hori spends a lot of time at school studying hieroglyphic writing, to learn how to read the language. The writing shown above is a mixture of sound signs and word signs.

The Egyptians have no written vowels, so many words look alike. To help tell them apart, they often write the sound of a word, then put a special sign, called a determinative, after it to make its meaning clearer.

This is what the writing shown above means:

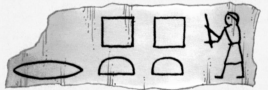

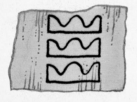

The word for "house" sounds like the word for "go forth", so the house symbol is used for both. The walking legs show that here it means "go forth".

The club is a sound sign which means "majesty". The snake is the Egyptian letter "f". But it can also be used to mean "his", as it does here.

The mouth is the sound sign for "r" and, also, the word for "to". The stool is the sound sign for "p", and the loaf of bread is the sign for "t". Repeated, they spell the word for "crush". To make the meaning of the word even clearer, a determinative sign for "force" – a man with a stick – is added on at the end.

As Egypt is flat, the sign for "hill" also means "foreign land". Here it is plural. So the sentence reads: "Goes forth His Majesty to crush foreign lands."

KEY   WORD SIGNS AND DETERMINATIVES   SOUND SIGNS

 (WALKING LEGS) GO

 (MAN WITH STICK) FORCE

 (HILLS) FOREIGN LAND

 (HOUSE) STANDS FOR "PR"

 (CLUB) STANDS FOR "HM"

 (HORNED VIPER) STANDS FOR "F"

 (MOUTH) STANDS FOR "R"

(STOOL) STANDS FOR "P"

(LOAF OF BREAD) STANDS FOR "T"

A TRIP TO THE PYRAMIDS

The pyramids were built over a thousand years before Nakht was born. They are very old, but they still look magnificent. They stand on the edge of the desert, across the Nile from Nakht's home.

During the flood season, the Nile rises close to the pyramids. Sightseers, like Nakht and his family, can sail up to them and pay their respects to the dead Pharaohs or visit the buildings.

HOW THE PYRAMIDS WERE BUILT

1. One way of cutting stone blocks for a pyramid was to cut notches in solid rock and hammer in wooden wedges. When water was poured on the wedges, they swelled, splitting off the blocks cleanly.

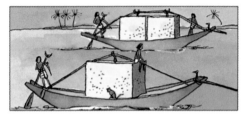

2. Most of the massive blocks used to build the Great Pyramid were quarried in the desert nearby. The white stones used to form the outer layer were brought across the Nile from the east bank.

3. The ground where the pyramid was to be built had to be cleared of sand and stones. Workers dug long channels and filled them with water. When the water didn't run to one end, they knew the site was level.

4. The most difficult job of all was to raise the heavy stones into place. Most people think the stones were pulled up a huge earth ramp that was raised each time a new layer of stones was added.

5. When the pyramid was finished, the ramp was taken away layer by layer. As the ramp went down, workers put white blocks of limestone on the jagged sides of the pyramid, to give them a smooth outer surface.

6. After many years' work, the pyramid was ready. When the Pharaoh died, his coffin was dragged up to the burial chamber inside it. Then the way into the pyramid was blocked with stone slabs and hidden.

INSIDE THE GREAT PYRAMID

The most impressive of all the pyramids is the Great Pyramid, built for Pharaoh Cheops. It is the biggest stone building ever built. Two million huge blocks of cut stone were used to construct it.

King Cheops had it made to keep his body safe after his death. He stocked the burial chamber with treasures to use in his afterlife

Despite his efforts, thieves found their way in to the pyramid. There is nothing left inside the pyramid but the stone coffin in which Cheops was buried.

SMALL PYRAMIDS FOR THE PHARAOH'S CHIEF QUEENS WERE BUILT BESIDE THE TOMB.

THIS CAUSEWAY LINKS THE MORTUARY TEMPLE TO A SECOND TEMPLE NEARER THE NILE.

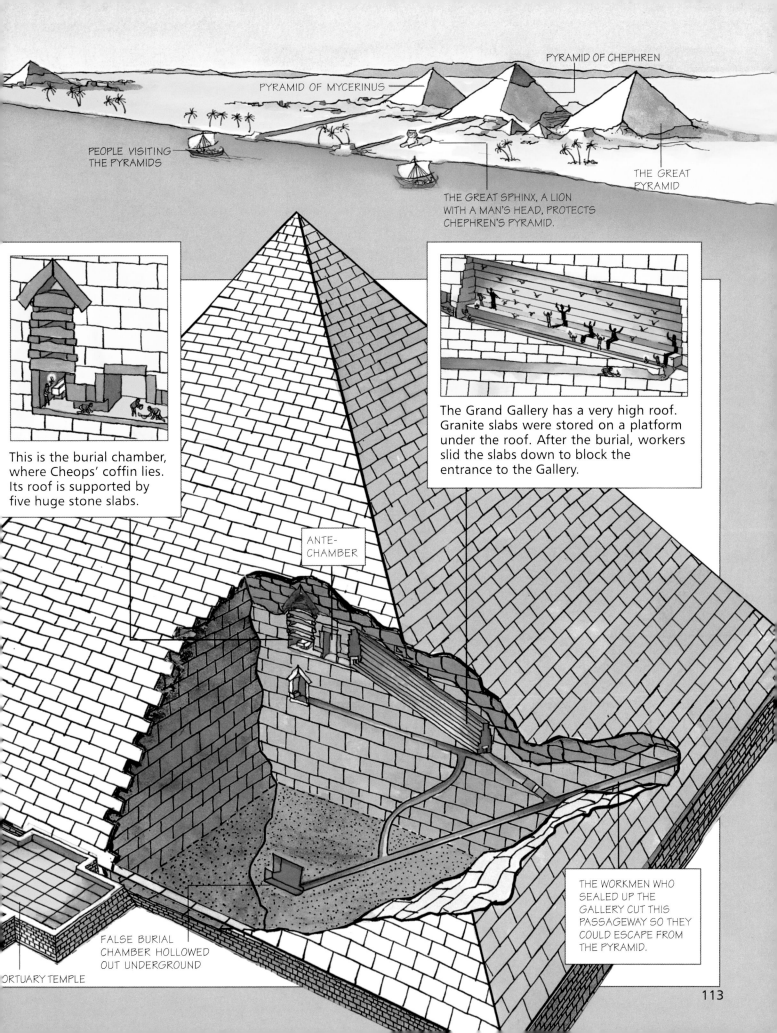

PYRAMID OF CHEPHREN

PYRAMID OF MYCERINUS

PEOPLE VISITING
THE PYRAMIDS

THE GREAT
PYRAMID

THE GREAT SPHINX, A LION
WITH A MAN'S HEAD, PROTECTS
CHEPHREN'S PYRAMID.

This is the burial chamber,
where Cheops' coffin lies.
Its roof is supported by
five huge stone slabs.

The Grand Gallery has a very high roof.
Granite slabs were stored on a platform
under the roof. After the burial, workers
slid the slabs down to block the
entrance to the Gallery.

ANTE-
CHAMBER

THE WORKMEN WHO
SEALED UP THE
GALLERY CUT THIS
PASSAGEWAY SO THEY
COULD ESCAPE FROM
THE PYRAMID.

FALSE BURIAL
CHAMBER HOLLOWED
OUT UNDERGROUND

ORTUARY TEMPLE

SETTING SAIL FOR THEBES

Today, Mosi is catching a boat. He must sail to Thebes to join his father, Nakht, who is on business at Pharaoh's court.

At the port, a boat has just arrived with a precious cargo of goods from a land named Punt.

The port is very busy. Some men are unloading the boat, while others note down its cargo. People are shopping. There is no money, so they exchange goods. This is called bartering. A group of bedouins have come from the desert to trade.

LEATHER WORKERS

POOR PEOPLE LIVE IN SMALL, CRAMPED HOUSES.

MOSI

BARBER

SCALES

STALL-KEEPERS ARE DOING GOOD BUSINESS.

PEOPLE WORK OUTSIDE BECAUSE IT IS SO HOT.

A BEDOUIN MAN WITH A BEARD AND BRIGHT CLOTHES

BEDOUINS' DONKEYS LADEN WITH DYED CLOTH TO EXCHANGE FOR FOOD

BOAT FROM PUNT
CARRYING A RICH CARGO

BABOONS

ELEPHANT TUSKS

AN APPRENTICE
MIXING CLAY

VENT TO
CATCH BREEZES

IN HOT WEATHER PEOPLE
SLEEP ON BEDROLLS ON
THE ROOFS

KILN FOR
BAKING
POTS

POTTERS
AT WORK

HOUSES, POTS AND
JARS ARE MADE
FROM NILE MUD.

115

AT PHARAOH'S COURT

Nakht is attending a reception at Pharaoh's palace in Thebes.

Ambassadors have come from Syria, a mountainous land northeast of Egypt. They are bringing gifts to Pharaoh. Some of these will go to Nakht's temple for the god Ptah. The gifts include a bear for the royal zoo. The Syrians also bring royal children who will stay at court. They will be treated well, but they are hostages who will be killed if their parents rebel.

Like all Egyptians, Nakht worships Pharaoh. He believes that Pharaoh is the son of the god Amun and that his word is law.

Young Pharaoh sits with his wife in the audience-hall. He is bored with the Syrian's flattery. He has heard news of a revolt in Kush. He is awaiting the arrival of his governor from Kush. Pharaoh knows that if there has been a revolt it will mean war.

PHARAOH AND HIS WIFE SIT ON A RAISED PLATFORM.

SYRIAN AMBASSADORS

A DAY IN THE LIFE OF PHARAOH

Pharaoh is dressed by his servants. They give him objects that are symbols of his royalty, a flail, a crook, and a headdress called a *nemes*.

Every morning in the temple, Pharaoh burns incense over a gift that has been offered to Amun. He asks the god to bring Egypt good luck.

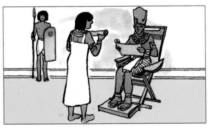

Much of the day is taken up governing the country. Pharaoh reads letters and consults his advisors. The Vizier helps to keep him informed.

THE CROWNS OF EGYPT

Pharaoh wears different crowns for different occasions. This is the blue war crown.

The White Crown is the crown of southern Egypt. The Red Crown is the crown of the Delta region.

As ruler of all Egypt, Pharaoh usually wears the Double Crown, which unites the Red and White.

The elaborate, top-heavy *hemhemet* crown is only worn for ceremonies at the temple.

COPPER

ROYAL CHILDREN

A TRUMPETER ANNOUNCES THE GOVERNOR'S ARRIVAL.

THE GOVERNOR OF KUSH ARRIVING WITH TWO LOYAL PRINCES FROM NUBIA

NAKHT

In the afternoon, Pharaoh goes to watch work on a temple he is having built for himself. Workers are hauling huge stone blocks into place.

Pharaoh loves hunting in the desert, but it can be dangerous. The fiercest prey are lions. In ten years Pharaoh has killed more than 100 lions.

Back in the palace, Pharaoh relaxes and plays a game of *senit* with his wife. The game is played on a board with 30 squares. Then Pharaoh goes to bed.

BATTLE!

The news from Kush is bad. Nubian tribesmen who live to the south of Egypt have rebelled. Pharaoh decides to send soldiers to punish them.

An expedition is organized quickly. Egypt has an army of trained soldiers. The most highly trained are charioteers, who provide their own chariots. Only a few of them will go to Kush, because it is difficult to carry horses down the Nile on boats.

One of the soldiers joining the expedition is Nakht's son Mosi. He is a new recruit and is eager to prove himself in battle.

1. PHARAOH CALLS HIS MEN TO ARMS

> Bring out the weapons so that the courage of my father Amun may humble the rebellious lands!

SCRIBE

BOWS

QUIVERS

WAR COUNCIL

SPEARS

AXES

While the soldiers receive their weapons for the battle, Pharaoh encourages them with a traditional battle cry.

2. THE EXPEDITION CAMPS BY THE NILE

The journey to the battlefield takes many days. The army has made camp on the way. Generals have their own tents, but the soldiers sleep in the open.

GUARDS

SOLDIERS WRESTLING

COOK

CAMP BED

Soldiers have to work long hours and often go hungry. If they make mistakes, they are beaten. But if they fight bravely, Pharaoh may reward them with farmland and foreign slaves.

3. ATTACK!

Archers begin the attack with a hail of arrows, then foot soldiers run forward. The Nubians are no match for the better armed Egyptians.

The battle is soon over. Chariots chase the survivors from the field.

4. SPOILS OF VICTORY

Nubian captives are led away into slavery. To check how many of the enemy are dead, scribes count piles of hands cut from dead warriors.

The Egyptian soldiers set fire to the Nubian camp, and steal their food and animal skins.

A WARRIOR IS BURIED

During the battle in Kush, some Egyptian soldiers were killed. One was Mosi's friend named Bata.

Bata's parents have brought his body to Thebes for burial. The funeral procession makes its way to a tomb on the west bank of the Nile. Four priests perform a burial ceremony.

THE TOMB HAS BEEN HOLLOWED OUT OF A CLIFF.

THIS PRIEST WEARS THE MASK OF THE JACKAL-HEADED GOD ANUBIS.

WOMEN MOURNERS HOWL AND THROW DUST OVER THEIR HEADS.

FOOD AND WINE FOR THE FEAST HELD AFTER THE BURIAL

BATA'S BODY INSIDE A MUMMY

THIS CHEST HOLDS JARS CONTAINING PARTS OF THE DEAD MAN'S BODY.

SOME MOURNERS ARE RELATIVES, OTHERS ARE PROFESSIONALS HIRED FOR THE FUNERAL.

PREPARING BATA FOR BURIAL

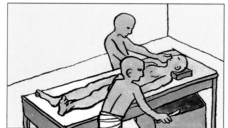

Men called embalmers try to preserve Bata's body for the after-life. They remove his brains and some internal organs. Then they clean his body and fill it with sweet-smelling spices.

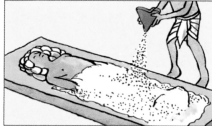

Next, they cover Bata's body with a kind of salt called natron. Bags of natron are packed around his head. Then the body is left for many days until all the moisture left in it has dried out.

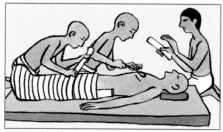

Bata's body is wrapped in linen bandages to make a "mummy". He is coated with oils and decorated with jewels and charms. A mask goes over Bata's face. Then he is wrapped again.

BATA'S BODY WAS TAKEN TO THE TOMB IN A BOAT.

THE BOAT WAS PULLED BY OXEN.

SLAVES CARRYING JEWELS, FURNITURE AND FOOD FOR BATA TO ENJOY IN HIS AFTERLIFE.

THE WORLD OF THE SPIRITS

Egyptian people believe in a life after death in which they will work, eat and drink just as they did on earth. Their tombs will be their homes, so wealthy people like Bata's parents take great care preparing their tombs.

Dead people must eat too, so piles of food are painted on tomb walls. People believe that the painted food will, by magic, stop them from being hungry.

Nakht is talking to his children about Bata's death, and his life after death in the world of the spirits.

When Bata died, his soul left his body in the shape of a bird. During the daytime, it flies back to the land of the living to revisit the places Bata knew when he was alive.

A MAP OF THE WORLD OF THE SPIRITS

Wealthy Egyptians have books, called Books of the Dead, put in their tombs. The books contain drawings of the Fields of Yaru – the Egyptian heaven. It is a peaceful land of fields, marshes and canals. After death, good people live there among the gods. They have to work in the fields. To avoid this, rich Egyptians put small statues called *ushabtis* in their tombs. They believe that the *ushabtis* will do the hard work for them.

RA, GOD OF THE SUN

Egyptians believe that each day the Sun travels across the sky in a boat guided by Ra, the falcon-headed god of the Sun. At night, Ra gets into another boat to sail with the Sun through the world of the spirits.

THE SUN

RA

BATA'S TRIP TO THE UNDERWORLD

1

2

Nakht tells his children about the frightening ordeal that dead Bata must face. Before he can live again in the world of the spirits, he must stand trial before Osiris, Lord of the Underworld. Only good people pass Osiris's test; the rest face a terrible fate.

The kingdom of Osiris lies in the West, where the Sun sets. The dead Bata has to travel there by boat. The snake goddess Meresger will go with him to protect him from serpents he may meet in the underworld.

To reach Osiris, Bata has to pass many gateways. Each one is guarded by animal-headed gods. These gods hold knives or feathers. The feathers represent truth. To pass through the gates, Bata must recite magic words written in his Book of the Dead.

3

In the judgement hall, which is called the Hall of the Two Truths, the dead Bata will meet Osiris. In front of Osiris and 42 judges, Bata must deny that he did any wrong in his life.

Jackal-headed Anubis is the god of the Dead. He will test Bata's claim by placing Bata's heart on a set of scales. On the other side of the scales, he places a feather of truth.

If Bata's heart is heavier than the feather, it means he has lied, and a beast called the Devourer will eat him. The beast is part lion, part crocodile and part hippopotamus.

4

Ibis-headed Thoth, the scribe of the gods, will note down the result of the trial. If it proves that Bata was a good man, he will be taken by the falcon-headed god Horus to the throne of Osiris, to worship him. Then, at last, Bata's new life in the Fields of Yaru will begin.

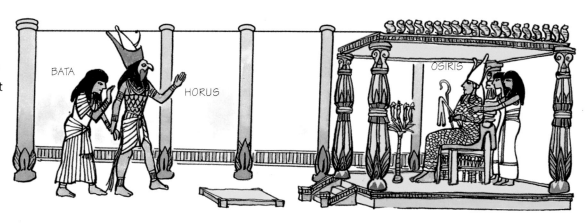

THE STORY OF THE PHARAOHS

The story begins in about 3100 BC, when Menes, a king from the south of Egypt (known as Upper Egypt) conquered the north of Egypt (known as Lower Egypt). He built a new capital city at Memphis, and ruled as the first of the Pharaohs.

MENES FIGHTS TO UNITE EGYPT

The first great pyramid was built 400 years later. It was a tomb for Pharaoh Zoser. Before this, Pharaohs were buried in flat-topped tombs called *mastabas*. Zoser's tomb looked like six *mastabas* on top of each other, and is known as the Step Pyramid.

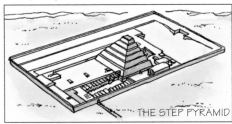
THE STEP PYRAMID

All the great pyramids were built over the next 400 years. The two biggest were built at Giza.

THE GREAT PYRAMIDS

The period when the pyramids were built is known as the Old Kingdom. Egypt was peaceful and grew rich. Peasants farmed the land and priests prayed, to the gods. The rich nobles served their Pharaoh, looked after their lands, and enjoyed hunting.

HUNTING

The nobles finally brought the Old Kingdom to an end. They grew so powerful that they no longer respected the Pharaohs at all. The country split in two and was ruled by rival kings, one in southern Egypt and one in the north.

WARRIORS

This unrest lasted for more than 150 years. It ended when a family who ruled Thebes managed to reunite the country. They crushed all opposition to their rule, and put Thebans in important government positions. They succeeded in restoring peace and limiting the power of the nobles. This new period of calm and prosperity is called the Middle Kingdom.

The Middle Kingdom was another great period for Egypt. Fine hieroglyphic writings were composed. Trading abroad increased. In the Delta and Nubia, chains of great fortresses were built to guard Egypt's borders. Marshes were drained in the Faiyum.

A FORTRESS

After 250 years of peace, civil war broke out again. Upper and Lower Egypt split. Foreigners, known as the Hyksos, conquered Lower Egypt. They used new weapons, including horses and chariots.

THE HYKSOS ATTACK

After a century, the rulers of Upper Egypt drove out the Hyksos. Thebes became the capital of a reunited Egypt. The Theban Pharaohs won back the country's earlier frontiers. Inside Egypt, order was restored.

During the first century of the New Kingdom, Egypt had its first truly powerful woman ruler. She was called Hatshepsut. At first, she ruled Egypt on behalf of her young stepson Tuthmosis III. Then she took all the power of a Pharaoh for herself. She ruled well for 20 years, and built a temple into the cliff face at Deir el Bahari, as a monument to herself.

DEIR EL BAHARI

As soon as Tuthmosis III took power, he tried to wipe out the memory of the woman who had stolen his throne. Then, he attacked Egypt's enemies abroad. In over 15 campaigns he built an empire that stretched from Syria to the Sudan.

TUTHMOSIS II

The empire survived until the end of the reign of Tuthmosis's great-grandson, Amenophis III. It crumbled under Amenophis's son, Akhenaten. He was the most revolutionary of Egypt's Pharaohs. He moved the capital of Egypt from Thebes to a new city which he called Akhetaten.

Above all, he tried to overthrow the old gods, and to replace them with only one god – Aten, the Sun's disc.

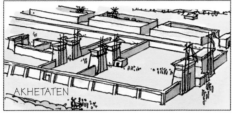
AKHETATEN

Akhenaten's efforts were in vain. During the reign of Tutankhamun, people began to worship all the other gods again. When Tutankhamun died at only 20 years old, his successors did their best to wipe Akhenaten's name from people's memories.

TUTANKHAMUN

Since Amenophis III's reign, Egypt's enemies abroad had been growing stronger. The last rulers of the New Kingdom struggled to keep them in check. After a long war, Rameses II signed a treaty with the Hittites, a people from what is now Turkey. In a great naval battle, Rameses III defeated the Sea Peoples of the Mediterranean.

RAMESES III'S BATTLE AT SEA

After Rameses III's death, Egypt was attacked by different groups of invaders. First came the Nubians and then the Assyrians sacked Thebes in 661 BC.

The Persians conquered Egypt next. The Egyptians hated the Persian people so much that when Alexander the Great of Greece invaded Egypt and defeated them, he was welcomed as a hero.

THE PERSIANS ATTACKING

After Alexander died, one of his generals, Ptolemy, took power. His family ruled Egypt for the next 300 years. Finally, Egypt became part of the Roman Empire. The last of the Pharaohs was Cleopatra. She killed herself with the venom of snake, rather than be ruled by the Roman Octavian.

CLEOPATRA DYING

The Ancient Egyptian way of life gradually disappeared. But its heritage has given much to the modern world, from building and farming to writing and science.

HOW WE KNOW ABOUT ANCIENT EGYPT

After Egypt became a part of the Roman Empire in 30 BC, its old way of life gradually came to an end. People began to worship new gods, and the secrets of hieroglyphic writing were forgotten. The old temples and palaces became ruins, and were covered with sand and rubble.

In the 18th century, Europeans visited Egypt and explored the ruined buildings. People eventually found out how to read hieroglyphic writing again.

Archeologists began to dig up the temples and tombs. They found wall paintings, scrolls and lots of objects used in daily life. People have used all these discoveries to build up a picture of how the Ancient Egyptians lived.

When archeologists found the temple of Abu Simbel, shown above, the great statues of Rameses II, for whom it was built, were covered in sand. The Europeans often damaged buildings when they were looking for treasure. Some even opened tombs with battering rams. Many things were taken back to Europe, like the sculpture of Rameses II shown below.

HOW THE HIEROGLYPHIC CODE WAS CRACKED

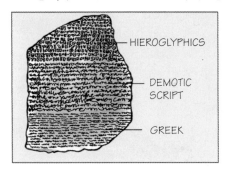

HIEROGLYPHICS

DEMOTIC SCRIPT

GREEK

The vital clue to the meaning of hieroglyphs was a stone dug up in 1799, near Rosetta, in the Delta. A message was written on it in Greek and in two kinds of Egyptian writing, demotic and hieroglyphic.

A French scholar called Jean-François Champollion compared the hieroglyphs with the Greek text, which he understood. He worked for 14 years before he made out the meaning of a single word.

PTOLMYS

KLEOPATRA

The first word he recognized was "Ptolemy", which was the name of the Greek Pharaohs. By comparing it with the spelling of "Cleopatra", he worked out the symbols for the letters "p", "l" and "o".

TUTANKHAMUN'S TOMB

The greatest discovery in the history of Egyptian archeology was finding the tomb of the young king Tutankhamun. Most of the Pharaoh's treasure was still inside the tomb, because grave robbers had been unable to find it.

The discovery was made by an English archeologist named Howard Carter. From what he knew about royal tombs, he was sure that there must still be one undiscovered tomb in the area known as the Valley of the Kings.

For five years he searched without finding anything. Then, on November 4, 1922, workers uncovered the first step of a flight of stone stairs while digging under a group of huts.

Carter and a colleague uncovering the entrance to Tutankhamun's tomb

Carter guessed at once that they had found what they had been looking for. Three weeks after the first step had been unearthed, Carter and his men uncovered the entrance to Pharaoh Tutankhamun's tomb.

Carter made an opening in the wall blocking the burial rooms and looked inside. Holding a candle through the hole, he peered into the darkness. "Can you see anything?" someone asked. "Yes", Carter replied. "Wonderful things."

Carter looking into Tutankhamun's burial chamber

Carter said that he could see "strange animals, statues and gold – everywhere the glint of gold." In the middle of the main room was a golden couch, shaped like a cow.

The archeologists found over 2,000 objects stored in four separate rooms. Many of them were made of gold. The mummy of the king's body was discovered inside a magnificent coffin.

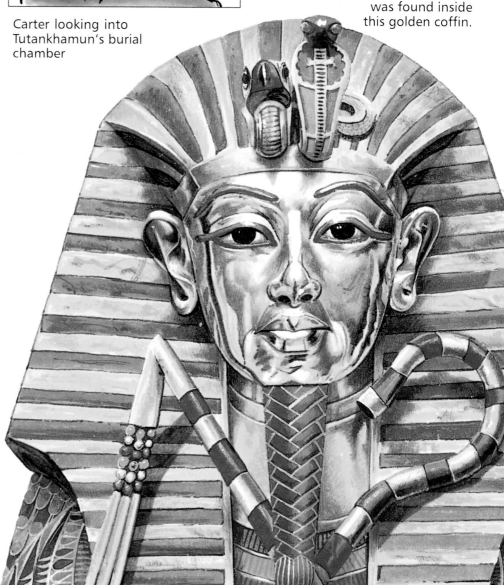

Tutankhamun's body was found inside this golden coffin.

PHARAOHS & PYRAMIDS TIME QUIZ

1. What would you expect to find in a catch-basin?
2. What is the name of the board game that Mosi and Ahmose like to play?
3. Who is the god of Memphis?
4. What does the hieroglyph sign ⊙ mean?
5. Approximately how many stone blocks were used to build the Great Pyramid for Cheops?
6. Which of his crowns does Pharaoh wear for ceremonies at the temple?
7. What is the name of the young soldier killed in Kush and buried in a tomb on the west bank of the Nile, near Thebes?
8. Who is the Lord of the Underworld?
9. What is the name of the beast that is part lion, part crocodile and part hippopotamus?
10. How did Cleopatra, the last of the Pharaohs, kill herself?

Answers on page 130.

INDEX

ACKNOWLEDGEMENTS

Knights & Castles – Usborne Publishing would like to thank the following historical consultants for their help with this book:
Peter Vansittart, a former teacher and a novelist with a special interest in the 13th century;
Angela Littler, who has written and edited several best-selling children's information books;
Nicholas Hall, who specializes in medieval architecture and weapons;
Gillian Evans, from the Medieval Centre at Reading University.
Additional illustrations on pages 5 and 19 by Joseph McEwan.
Pharoahs & Pyramids – This book was prepared in consultation with W.V. Davies, Assistant Keeper of Egyptian Antiquities for the British Museum, and Dr. Anne Millard, author of several books and articles on Ancient Egypt for children.
Tutankhamun's coffin illustration on page 127 by Ian Jackson.

First published in 1977 and revised in 1998 by Usborne Publishing Ltd,
83-85 Saffron Hill, London EC1N 8RT, England.
Copyright © 1976, 1978, 1990, 1993, 1997, 1998 Usborne Publishing Ltd.
The name Usborne and the device ⊕ are Trade Marks of Usborne Publishing Ltd.
All rights reserved. No part of this publication may be reproduced, stored in a retrieval system, or transmitted in any form or by any means, electronic, mechanical, photocopying, recording or otherwise, without the prior permission of the publisher.
First published in America in 1999. Printed in Belgium. UE.

ANSWERS TO THE TIME QUIZZES

Answers to the quiz on page 32:
1. The keep
2. Three prisoners
3. A troubadour
4. Coins
5. Apprentices
6. A pilgrim
7. He is a dentist and a surgeon
8. A rotating target for knights to practice using a lance.
9. Coats-of-arms
10. Jerusalem

Answers to the quiz on page 64:
1. The longhouse
2. A container in which barley is ground into flour
3. Their sea chests
4. A golden cross
5. Runes
6. The god of Thunder
7. Hedeby
8. A meeting at which Vikings discuss business matters and the law
9. Four deer and four rabbits
10. Rune stones

Answers to the quiz on page 96:
1. The Tiber River
2. An open square in a town
3. A toga
4. A hypocaust
5. Gladiators
6. The Colosseum
7. Seven times
8. Water
9. Their fingers
10. The pattern in which Roman soldiers linked their shields together to protect themselves

Answers to the quiz on page 128:
1. Flood water
2. Senit
3. Ptah
4. Sun
5. Two million
6. The hemhemet
7. Bata
8. Osiris
9. The Devourer
10. With the venom of a snake